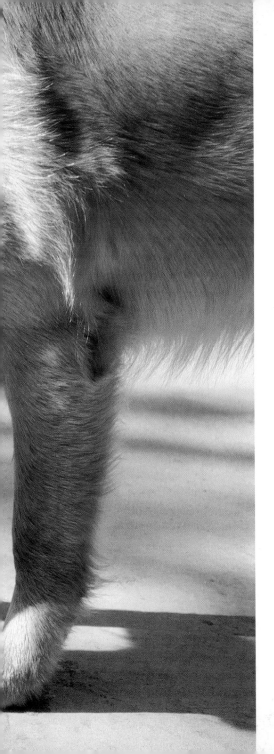

Cheryl S. Smith

Pudgy Pooch, Picky Pooch

A Pet Owner's Guide to Dog Food and Canine Nutrition

With 71 photographs
Illustrations by Tana Herkanson Monsalve

D1410227

BARRON'S

Important Note

Each individual pet is unique and it is impossible to diagnose problems simply from reading a book. Always consult your veterinarian before administering any type of treatment, supplement, or medication to your pet. If the information and procedures contained in this book differ in any way from your veterinarian's recommendations concerning your pet's health care, please consult him or her prior to their implementation. Nutrition is a complex subject. This book presents the basics of the most up-to-date information, but research is unending and new discoveries are made all the time. As not all veterinarians are well-versed in the subject of nutrition, you may want to discuss some of the questions raised here with this book in hand. The health and well-being of your dog are always the best indication of good or poor nutrition.

About the Author

Cheryl S. Smith is a member of the Dog Writers Association of America, the Association of Pet Dog Trainers, the Cat Writers Association, and the Author's Guild. She has written professionally for television, stage, newspapers, magazines, and book publishers. As a freelance writer with 15 years of experience, she has conducted extensive research on animal-related topics with veterinarians, trainers, and other experts. She is hopelessly in love with dogs—all sorts and sizes of dogs—but is also a soft touch for everything from finches to cats to fish to sheep. She is always experimenting with training new species in new ways, and is currently involved in teaching a matched pair of sheep to pull a cart. She lives on the Olympic Peninsula with two dogs, three sheep, pond fish, and an immense flock of wild ducks.

Other Barron's titles by Cheryl S. Smith
The Trick Is in the Training (1998)

Photo Credits

Adlard Photographers: pages 18, 41, 43, 105, 124; Norvia Behling: cover, inside front cover, inside back cover, back cover; Paulette Braun: pages 4, 93, 151; Donna Coss: page 120; Kent and Donna Dannen: pages 2, 35, 77, 123, 128; Bonnie Nance: pages 48, 53, 84; Dee Ross: pages 62, 63; Bob Schwartz: pages 107, 147; Cheryl S. Smith: pages 1, 13, 14, 19, 21, 24, 26, 28, 34, 36, 50, 55, 56, 59, 67, 74, 86, 111, 129, 133, 144, 145, 158, 159; Sherry Smith: pages vi, 100; Judith Strom: pages 20, 22, 52, 89, 94, 97, 104, 106, 109, 110, 119, 140, 164, 167; Toni Tucker: page 114; Paola Visintini: page 153; Waltham Centre for Pet Nutrition: page 3; Janet York: page 125; Missy Yuhl: pages 31, 101.

All inquiries should be addressed to:
Barron's Educational Series, Inc.
250 Wireless Boulevard
Hauppauge, New York 11788
http://www.barronseduc.com

International Standard Book No. 0-7641-0289-3

Library of Congress Catalog Card No. 98-2868

Library of Congress Cataloging-in-Publication Data

Smith, Cheryl, 1949-
    Pudgy pooch, picky pooch : a pet owner's guide to dog food and canine nutrition / Cheryl S. Smith ; illustrations by Tana Hakanson Monsalve.
        p.   cm.
    Includes bibliographical references (p. 172) and index.
    ISBN 0-7641-0289-3
    1. Dogs—Food. 2. Dogs—Nutrition. I. Title.
    SF427.4.S56   1998
    636.7'08'5—dc21   98-2868
                                                    CIP

Printed in Hong Kong

987654321

Contents

Preface

Nutrition is a complex and ever-evolving subject. New foods were being introduced and official opinions about artificial preservatives were being changed even as this book was being written. However, the information included in these pages will give you a serious grounding in just what your dog needs and how to go about finding it.

Though specific pet food companies are sometimes mentioned in the book, no actual recommendation by product name is made anywhere in these pages. Instead, the information you need to make an educated choice is provided. Selection of brand and formulation is left to you. This book does not contain any "just for fun" exercises that have your dog do taste testing or any cute illustrations. In fact, this subject can be heavy going at times. But if you want a book about canine nutrition, then the book should deliver information on canine nutrition. This one does.

I would like to thank veterinarians Dennis Wilcox and James Sokolowski, both of whom read the manuscript and made helpful suggestions, often sending me down further paths of research. Susan Roush at GCI Spindler was most helpful in obtaining research materials and artwork for the book. Jo Wills at Waltham Centre for Pet Nutrition, AAFCO Secretary R. J. Noel, Kerry Lyman and Jennifer Condren at Ralston Purina, Beth White and Bryan Brown at Iams, and Hilda Donohue at the British Small Animal Veterinary Association all provided books, tables, charts, and the permissions to use them. David Dzanis at the FDA submitted to a long interview and was most gracious in his assistance. Local stores—Paws & Fins of Sequim, Baxter Farms of Port Angeles, and Four-Legged Friends of Port Townsend—allowed photographs to be taken in their stores and chatted about dog food. Hurricane Ridge Kennel Club unwittingly timed their first ever AKC-approved dog show just enough days before deadline to allow some of the thousands of dogs entered to be photographed. Mary Falcon, my editor at Barron's, and the anonymous reviewers provided valuable tips to make this difficult subject more accessible to you, the reader. Judy Winthrop had the stamina to read several versions of the manuscript and suggest ways it could be friendlier and less technical. Her support as the deadline neared and the book grew ever longer was invaluable. Sundance, Spirit, and

Serling were, throughout their lives, willing subjects for testing any foods or treats. They provided valuable experience by being allergic to corn, having delicate digestion, and suddenly rejecting random substances.

In case any reader is interested, the author daily feeds her dogs a super-premium dry food moistened with homemade chicken broth with the fat skimmed off. Her dog's coats have been widely admired and exclaimed over. Her dogs have lived to be 11 (Keeshond), 16 (springer mix), and 15 and still counting (Newfoundland mix).

Chapter One
The History of Dog Food

It was probably food that brought us together in the first place. The theory suggests that some 25,000 years ago, wolves were attracted to the kills made by early humans. As the wolves hung around to scavenge remains, a sort of accidental domestication occurred. The wolf-dogs had sharper senses and could warn humans of approaching danger. The humans shared their food, shelter, and company. Over long years, the wolf became the dog. Alternate theories suggest that a combination of the jackal, hyena, and wolf may be the dog's ancestor. We'll probably never know. The important thing is that the wild canine became *Canis familiaris*, the dog.

The food relationship remained unchanged for many, many years. Dogs were fed whatever humans had to offer. In the far north, this was and often still is dried fish. For the Mayans, it was meat mixed with corn. Across much of the farmlands of Europe and later America it was a combination of the bread, potatoes, milk, cottage cheese, and eggs most readily available to the farm families. Most

dogs hunted or scavenged to supplement their diets. Though humans now find it distasteful, dogs got a good dose of vitamins and minerals by eating the output of grass-eating animals (cow pies and other such delicacies) and the entrails of whatever kills they made on their own. These natural, close-to-the-earth diets of unprocessed

Whether descended from the wolf, jackal, fox, or hyena, the dog is now our intimate companion.

Sled dogs, from Admiral Byrd's expedition to today's racing competitors and weight pullers, require optimum nutrition.

have been subjected to inferior nutrition by their doting owners. Prince Albert fed his treasured greyhound fresh butter and pâté de foie gras. The Pekingese of China was an Imperial dog indeed, and the Emperor Tz'u Hsi instructed "Shark's fin, and curlew's livers and the breasts of quail, on these it may be fed."

The Beginnings of Popularity

Canine cuisine began to change in the 1900s. Our own food was becoming more processed and packaged, especially in the cities. There weren't as many scraps, and the available ones weren't as nutritious. Some people bought scraps from a nearby slaughterhouse, some bought horsemeat, and some began to buy canned dog food.

In 1902, the Robinson-Danforth Commission Company in St. Louis changed its name to Ralston Purina. "Dr. Ralston" was a popular health guru at the time, who endorsed the company's cereal products. The Purina stood for the company slogan, "Where purity is paramount." Company leader William H. Danforth originated the checkerboard logo by dressing himself and his children in checked suits all cut from the same bolt of cloth. St. Louis trolley tour guides still remark on what a sight the family must have been seated in the front pew in church.

reindeer and rice, wild boar and corn, and fish and potatoes may not have been perfect nutrition, but they were good enough to keep much of the dog population in reasonably good health.

Efforts at marketing dog food began as early as 1870. Spratt's Patent Meat Fibrine Dog Cakes, a hard biscuit, was produced in England in that year. Their advertising claimed the product was "supplied to the Royal kennels," which is pretty clever, since all that says is they took some of their product to the royal pooches, not that any was actually fed to the dogs. James Spratt was actually an American living in London, and he soon began selling his products in the United States as well. Spratt's prospered enough to advertise on the covers of early copies of the *AKC Gazette*. However, most family dogs were fed family leftovers.

The early exceptions were mainly royal dogs, and they may actually

The Purina Pet Care Center opened in Gray Summit in 1926. That makes it, as the company proudly proclaims, the oldest research facility exclusively devoted to studying dog and cat growth, reproduction, maintenance, palatability, digestion, and management. Little was known about the nutrient requirements of dogs and cats. Early pet foods were commonly labeled *dog and cat diets* and fed to both.

Purina gained some real exposure in 1933 when Admiral Byrd took along Dog Chow Checkers to feed his sled dogs on his expedition to the South Pole. Byrd even named an Antarctic peak Mount Danforth in honor of Purina's leader.

Other companies started joining the competition. In 1932, Friskies opened their own pet care research facility at Carnation Farms northeast of Seattle. In England, Forrest Mars established a confectionary business that same year and three years later, acquired Chappel Brothers, a Manchester firm producing a canned meat for dogs—Ken-L Ration. The product was renamed Chappie, and is indisputably Britain's oldest pet food. Samuel Gaines broke into the dog food market with a new type of food called a "meal," a variety of dried ground ingredients mixed together and sold in 100-pound bags. Also in 1935, Friskies introduced the product Friskies Cubes, the first dry dog food to promote the concept of a complete and balanced pet food.

For the first 30 to 40 years of the twentieth century, pet foods were sold only in feed stores. The National Biscuit Company (now known as Nabisco) purchased Milk Bone in 1931 and promptly began efforts to sell its product in grocery stores. This idea met with strong resistance. Pet foods, made largely of by-products of foods meant for humans, were considered unsanitary. However, with persistence, Milk Bones made their appearance in the supermarket. The savings in time and money of being able to pur-

The Waltham Centre for Pet Nutrition in England houses a variety of dog breeds from toys to giants.

chase pet food right along with the family's food soon overcame any consumer reluctance. By the mid-1930s, a variety of pet food brands were being sold in grocery stores.

The new foods caught on first in urban areas. City dogs were eating canned food that resembled corned beef hash or dry foods shaped like biscuits or chunks. Their country cousins were still eating scraps and things like "yellow dog bread," a stiff slurry of cornmeal, flour, spoiled milk, bacon pan drippings, and maybe an egg or two.

Quality was not always reliable. While the larger companies were establishing research kennels and seriously investigating canine nutrition, others were simply trying to make a buck. During the Depression, the idea of turning cast-off by-products into a product for sale was irresistible. Grains left over from the manufacture of livestock feeds were combined with offal (intestines, brains, etc.) or even rotten meat and sold as dog food.

Canned foods became jarred foods as World War II demanded all available metals. Chappie was sold in glass jars from 1939 to 1953. Dry foods became more popular than canned for the first time (though canned foods resumed first place once the war was over). But even with continuing post-war shortages, the 1940s were a big time for dog food. Iams began in 1946 when Paul Iams decided that he wanted to produce the finest quality pet food. An early guide dog for the blind, Buddy, inspired formation of another pet food company. Buddy fell ill in 1948 and veterinary surgeon Mark Morris became the first to treat a dog by changing the dog's diet. Dr. Morris decided he could help Buddy's failing kidneys by reducing the levels of protein and minerals in his diet. Buddy improved dramatically, and Hill's Science Diet was born. Fromm Pet Foods also sprang to public attention in the 1940s with an all-granular food using a unique method of vitamin and mineral supplementation.

By 1947, Purina Chow brand foods, including both livestock and pet foods, accounted for $190 million of the company's total sales of $208 million. In 1951, sales of Mars' Foods' Chappie reached one million dollars. The company transferred to the tiny town of Melton Mowbray to increase production capacity. Soon they were churning out dog food around-the-clock seven days a week.

In the 1950s and 1960s, pet food really came into its own. Consumers who only a few years before had scoffed at the idea of paying for special foods when table scraps were available for free now couldn't live without the convenience of packaged foods. Health and nutrition were also becoming hot topics, and pet owners extended their own concerns to encompass their dogs and cats. Food choices for pets were increasingly varied, with more variety in ingredients and in forms. Canned foods continued to be popular, dry foods now made gravy when mixed with water, and soft moist packaged foods came along.

A Purina product with the code name X-24 was pressure-processed and extruded in a new method that became the basis for dry foods. This introduction of the new Dog Chow was so successful that the company simply couldn't make enough, and the product had to be rationed to the grocery stores where it was sold.

Extrusion involves mixing all of the food ingredients together then forcing the mixture through a tube under pressure in the presence of steam, thereby cooking the mixture. The resulting bite-sized food particles were more digestible than previous products, and a spraying of fat or other flavor enhancers as a coating made them highly palatable. In only one year, Purina Dog Chow became the best-selling dog food in the United States. The majority of dry pet foods today are extruded.

In England, 1960 saw the sale of the first cans of Pedigree Chum, Britain's most exclusive pet food. The price was a whopping ten pence a can. Acceptance came fast when the winners of Crufts, Britain's prestigious and the world's biggest dog show, began a long-standing association with Pedigree. The 1964 Best in Show winner, an English Setter named Silbury Soames, was the first champion fed Chum. Since then, more than two dozen supreme champions have followed the setter in feasting on Chum on their way to the top.

Companies in the United States are mainly identifiable under the same name through much of their history. Name recognition seems to be an important consideration. However, in England the story is harder to follow. Chappel Brothers became Mars became Petfoods Ltd., which then changed to Waltham and finally decided on Pedigree Petfoods Ltd., except that the research part of the company is still known as Waltham. In fact, the Waltham Centre for Pet Nutrition opened in 1965 and continues to use that name.

By the 1960s, dog foods had joined fast-food restaurants and TV dinners in offering convenience. In scarcely 30 years, attitudes had changed from laughing at the idea of spending money on dog food to total acceptance. Americans were spending $700 million a year on pet foods, more than they were spending on baby food.

Competition and Regulation

New companies continued to spring into existence. In 1972, nearly 1,500 brands of canned, dry, frozen, and moist packaged dog foods were available around the world. With increased competition, companies increased their advertising in the ongoing fight for market share. Purina passed former market leader Gaines and consolidated its position with the slogan, "All You Add Is Love."

Nature's Recipe began as one man's search for the answer to the terrible skin problems being suffered by his Samoyed. A veterinarian finally hypothesized that the dog was allergic to meat and helped owner Jeffrey Bennett formulate a home-cooked vegetarian diet. The diet was successful, and Bennett began marketing nonmeat dog kibble. He followed that with the first lamb and rice formulation. Lamb and rice has now become so popular that it is regularly fed to a wide population of dogs and has lost much of its effectiveness as a *hypoallergenic* (more correctly, novel foods) diet.

Today, in the intense fight for supermarket shelves, pet food often takes up more space than the seemingly endless sea of breakfast cereals. Owners are now demanding optimum nutrition. Super-premium foods have become the new leaders in the ever-expanding pet food industry.

As pet foods became big business, regulation became a concern. The quality of many early products was questionable, even deleterious.

Now, pet foods are regulated by a variety of agencies, though enforcement of regulations is not always a high priority with these multitasked government organizations. In the United States, pet foods are subject to federal, state, and local laws, including the Federal Food, Drug, and Cosmetic Act, the Fair Packaging and Labeling Act, USDA inspections, and more.

The Food and Drug Administration (FDA) specifies the ingredients permitted in pet foods and the acceptable manufacturing procedures. Inspection of facilities is usually relegated to state feed control officials. A department of the FDA, the Center for Veterinary Medicine (CVM), regulates any health claims made on pet food labels. Any health statement considered a drug claim renders the food subject to the FDA drug approval process. Some claims, such as hypoallergenic, are specifically disallowed.

The U.S. Department of Agriculture (USDA) requires that pet foods be clearly labeled so they cannot be mistaken for foods meant for human consumption. The USDA is responsible for inspecting and regulating research facilities. The physical structure, sanitation, housing, and care of the animals must be certified. For feeding trials to be meaningful, the testing facilities must be sanitary and provide proper care for the kennel dogs.

The National Research Council (NRC) is a private, nonprofit institution, the working arm of the National Academy of Sciences, National Academy of Engineering, and Institutes of Medicine. It collects and evaluates research conducted by others, in service to the federal government, the scientific community, and the general public. A standing committee on animal nutrition reviews reports and recommends appointments of scientists to subcommittees. The NRC made its last recommendations on the nutrient requirements for dogs and cats in 1985 and 1986. But because these recommendations were based mainly on purified or semipurified diets, with nutrients in highly available forms, they didn't really apply to the manufacturing of pet food. Pet food manufacturers were using the 1974 and 1978 NRC recommended allowances. In 1991, the NRC officially requested that their guidelines no longer be used to evaluate nutritional adequacy of dog and cat foods.

The Association of American Feed Control Officials (AAFCO) took over the development of nutrient profiles used as standards for the manufacture of pet foods. AAFCO is an association of state and federal feed control officials, not an official regulatory body, so its policies must be voluntarily accepted by state feed control officials. Though all states generally follow AAFCO guidelines, not all of them have mechanisms for actual inspection and enforcement. In addition to nutrient profiles, AAFCO specifies labeling procedures, ingredient nomenclature, and definitions.

The Pet Food Institute (PFI), a trade organization representing manufacturers of pet foods, works closely with AAFCO to evaluate current regulations and make recommendations for changes. The PFI also developed the Nutrition Assurance Program. This voluntary self-enforcement program was meant to be an additional way of verifying the nutritional adequacy of pet foods. To achieve NAP certification, the pet food manufacturer must subject the most basic of their nutritional formulations to AAFCO feeding trials plus digestibility trials and laboratory analysis. Unfortunately, this program has not achieved a high level of participation, and it may not continue. Although NAP certification information is not permitted on labels, the Pet Food Institute answers questions about specific pet foods and NAP certification at a toll-free number (1-800-851-0769).

In Canada, the Canadian Veterinary Medical Association (CVMA) administers the voluntary pet food certification program. To achieve initial certification, a product must be tested through both feeding trials and laboratory analysis. After passing initial certification, production is monitored every two months, and digestibility studies are conducted every six months. Currently, AAFCO does not permit the CVMA seal to appear on Canadian pet foods shipped to the United States for sale.

In Europe, the legislation controlling pet foods also covers feeds for farm animals raised for human consumption. Because they cover part of the human food chain, the regulations are strict. Most originate in European Community (EC) directives and are implemented through national regulations. In the United Kingdom, the Feeding Stuffs Regulations are the actual enforced directives. The directives cover such topics as marketing of compound feeding stuffs (mixtures of products of vegetable and animal origin), additives in feeding stuffs, undesirable substances (setting maximum permitted levels), and assessment. Voluntary organizations also exist such as the U.K. Pet Food Manufacturers' Association.

Chapter Two

All Dogs Are Not Created Equal

Only among dogs and horses can you find such remarkable size extremes within a single species. The comparison of Shetland pony to Clydesdale or Chihuahua to Irish Wolfhound is certainly striking. Amid dogs, there are also remarkable variances in body type (picture a Corgi and a Greyhound) and haircoat (between Beagles and Old English Sheepdogs, say). Factor in differences in temperament and the external environment, and you can begin to see the many potential influences on nutritional needs. Life stage and activity level are also instrumental in determining the optimum calories and levels of specific nutrients per day. But in one area, healthy dogs in general are pretty much the same—in their digestion and absorption of the food they eat.

Canine Digestion

Food is actually a combination of organic and inorganic components, many in the form of large molecules. These must be broken down or *degraded* to simpler substances before they can be of use to the body. This process of degradation is what makes up the actual digestion process. The passage of nutrients from the digestive tract (specifically the small intestine) to other body systems is the process of absorption.

The dog, in common with humans and pigs, is a *monogastric omnivore*, meaning the dog has one stomach and consumes a variety of animal and plant tissues. (Yes, the dog is commonly referred to as a carnivore. However, comparing the dog's teeth with the cat's shows that the dog has molars for chewing at least a small quantity of vegetable matter while the cat does not. The cat must eat animal protein to receive its nutrient requirements, while the dog can survive as a vegetarian.)

Digestion involves a combination of mechanical, chemical, and microbial activities, all serving to further degrade the food components. Digestion occurring in the dog's mouth is mainly mechanical. *Mastication* (chewing) breaks down large fragments and mixes them with

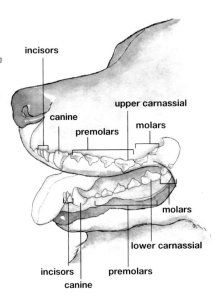

incisors

upper carnassial

canine

molars

premolars

molars

lower carnassial

incisors

premolars

canine

saliva. Canine saliva acts strictly as a lubricant, being 99 percent water and only 1 percent mucus with some inorganic salts and enzymes. It completely lacks the starch-digesting enzyme *amylase*, present in human saliva. This lack of digestive process in the mouth is one reason dogs can swallow their food whole (*bolt*) without ill effects. In fact, food swallowed in large chunks may actually be digested better because it remains in the stomach longer. (This lack of amylase in saliva also accounts for the relative lack of canine cavities.)

From the mouth, the food goes through the esophagus, a short muscular tube leading to the stomach. Food may be further mechanically broken down and mixed while descending the esophagus. A ring of specialized muscle cells at the entrance to the stomach (the *cardiac sphincter*) relaxes in response to the swallowing of food, allowing the food to pass into the stomach.

The stomach begins the chemical digestive process. It secretes acid and the precursor to the important enzyme pepsin, which starts protein digestion and plays a role in intestinal absorption of calcium, iron, and vitamin B12. The gastric muscles mix the food and the gastric juices into a semifluid mass called *chyme*. When the chyme is the correct viscosity, it is allowed to pass through the *pyloric sphincter*, another ring of muscles, and enter the small intestine.

Here is where the majority of chemical digestion occurs. The small in small intestine refers to its narrow diameter, not its length, which is considerable. Length is important. It directly impacts the amount of time food spends in the small intestine and thus the time available for digestion to take place. The ratio of the dog's small intestine length to body length is five to one, the same as in humans. The cat's ratio is three to one, the shorter intestine befitting the shorter digestive time of a carnivorous diet. The small intestine is made even larger by its interior, which is folded into small fingerlike projections called *microvilli*. This increases the surface area available for absorption.

Glands in the walls of the small intestine and in the pancreas secrete enzymes responsible for digesting fats, carbohydrates, and proteins. The pancreas also secretes large

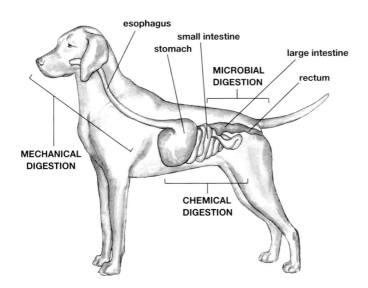

esophagus

small intestine

stomach

large intestine

MICROBIAL
DIGESTION

rectum

MECHANICAL
DIGESTION

CHEMICAL
DIGESTION

The canine digestive system.

amounts of bicarbonate salts to neutralize the acidity of the chyme and establish the correct pH (acid/alkaline level) for the enzymes to function best. Bile, produced in the liver and stored in the gallbladder, is mainly responsible for emulsifying the fats in the diet. The degraded food substances are absorbed by transferring from the small intestine to the blood or lymphatic system for delivery to the tissues.

Water is essential for digestion. The average dog weighing 45 pounds absorbs about three quarts of water a day. The digestive enzymes are secreted in a solution of water for better dispersion among food particles. Much digestion actually occurs through hydrolysis, the splitting of compounds by water. The elimination of toxins created in the digestion process via the kidneys also requires water.

Herbivores such as horses have really large large intestines to digest the vegetable matter that comprises much of their diet. But in dogs (and cats and humans), the large intestine is large in diameter but short in length. It consists of the cecum, colon, and rectum, all with relatively flat surfaces. The organic matter delivered to the large intestine is mostly dietary starches plus some undigested carbohydrates and proteins.

The chief function of the large intestine is to absorb water, salt, and electrolytes. But bacterial colonies in the large intestine do perform some microbial digestion on the arriving materials, producing the short-chain fatty acids *acetate, butyrate*, and *proprionate*. These volatile fatty acids are now thought to provide energy for the enzyme-producing intestinal wall and to contribute to intestinal health.

Fermentation by these bacterial colonies also leads to the production of gases. The amount of gases produced depends both on the dietary composition and the number and type of bacteria present. Certain types of carbohydrates found in legumes (such as soybeans) are relatively resistant to digestion by the enzymes in the small intestine. When these carbohydrates reach the colon, they are attacked by the bacterial colony, and intestinal gases are produced. This high level of gases results in flatulence—definitely one of the complaints about diets featuring soy.

Eating to Live, or Living to Eat

In nutrition, individuality is paramount. No one diet is going to be right for all dogs, all Shetland Sheepdogs, or even all Shetland Sheepdogs aged five weighing 25 pounds who walk a mile each day. Optimum nutrition is achieved with energy balance.

Energy balance is achieved by balancing input and output over long periods of time. The dog has both internal and external controls to encourage or discourage eating.

In mammals in general, the natural state of the body is hunger. This state can be *checked* or temporarily turned off by the presence of food in the gastrointestinal tract and the amount of nutrients being absorbed

or stored in the body. Changes in blood nutrient levels can signal neural and hormonal activity that will either initiate or inhibit eating. The stomach also plays a part. The contractions of an empty stomach result in a sensation of hunger and encourage eating, while distension of the stomach after a full meal definitely inhibits eating.

External controls are more individualized. They may include palatability of the diet, texture of the food, the timing of meals, and *social facilitation*.

Dogs have definite individual preferences, with favorite foods ranging from grapes to artichoke to chestnuts to cheese. However, in general and in terms of commercial foods, taste tests conducted by pet food manufacturers found that most dogs prefer canned and semimoist foods to dry food, favor beef as the preferred type of meat, choose warm food over cold, and show definite preference for cooked over uncooked meat. This doesn't mean that your dog will necessarily belong to the majority in all aspects.

Social facilitation is based on the dog's wild heritage. When a pack of wolves kills a large animal, the abundance of food and actions of other pack members eating encourages gorging. Our dogs tend to react in the same way. A dog who's a picky pooch as an only dog may become a robust eater when another dog is brought into the household. Dogs who consider their human family as their pack have a natural tendency to want to eat when their pack is eating, and so may beg at the table.

The timing and frequency of meals can also influence consumption. Many dogs fed free choice (food available at all times) will efficiently balance their intake with their actual energy needs and remain lean, but others will consistently overeat and will gain weight. Several controlled-portion meals a day seems to be the most efficient plan and relates well to the wild canine's preference of eating a number of small meals throughout the day. An Iams study showed that dogs fed four times a day increased their metabolism twice as much as dogs fed the same amount of food in one meal.

Another option employed by some dog owners is a cafeteria style diet. This involves frequently offering new types of food and giving of different sorts of treats, often including table scraps. These highly palatable novel foods can override the normal signals of satiety and encourage the dog to overeat.

At the other end of the scale, picky dogs, just like picky humans, may suddenly reject a food if they happened to eat it during or just before an illness.

Whether your pooch is picky or voracious, the amount of energy that should be consumed each day is determined by the amount of energy expended each day. No recommended range of energy requirements exists. There is, instead, a specific daily amount in response to

Good nutrition results in shiny coats, sparkling eyes, and general well-being.

daily circumstances. Many factors enter into the ever-changing energy requirements, as mentioned in the opening paragraph of this chapter.

In Sickness and In Health

For healthy dogs, one of the determinants of energy requirements is life stage. We will discuss this in detail in Chapter Nine and just give a quick overview here.

The life stages are growth (puppies), maintenance (adults), gestation and lactation (pregnant and nursing bitches), and senior (older than some age, generally seven, but

During hunting season or field trials, sporting dogs like this Vizsla may need a high-performance food.

nutrition isn't simply a matter of stuffing dogs with as much food as they'll eat—too much nutrition can have serious consequences, especially for puppies. Read Chapter Nine for full details.

Environmental conditions can also play a large role in determining caloric requirements. A dog in an outdoor kennel in a northern winter will nearly double his or her daily caloric intake, to burn for the *adaptive thermogenesis* (literally, heat generation) required to keep warm. Keep in mind that the dog actually has to be out in the weather. A dog all snug in a cozy 70-degree house does not need more food just because the weather outside is frightful.

And what about those working dogs? Again, we'll talk more about this in Chapter Nine, but note that a dog out herding, hunting, or pulling sleds all day may require four times the daily calories of a more sedentary individual. When the calories are consumed is also important for these dogs, and water consumption is critical.

Good nutrition is a major factor in keeping a dog healthy. The immune system requires good nutrition to be in optimum working order. Studies have shown that good nutrition actually boosts resistance to bacterial infections and parasitic infestations. The skin and haircoat, composed mainly of protein cells, are excellent indicators of a dog's overall health. Coats should be uniform and glossy, free from flakes or scales from the

varying by breed and individual). The category *working* or *performance* is frequently added, though not strictly a life stage.

Nutritional requirements can vary greatly depending solely on life stage. Puppies may require twice the daily caloric intake per pound of body weight as adults. Lactating bitches may need three times their normal calories per day to provide nourishment for both themselves and their puppies (even more if the litter is particularly large). However,

skin. Dry brittle coats and flaking skin can indicate either food-based nutritional problems or some disease process robbing the body of nutrients.

Diseases have serious impacts on nutritional requirements. One pet food manufacturer notes in a product brochure that "Nutrition is the foundation for all healing." No medical condition benefits from starvation. Proper nutritional support increases wound strength, and promotes wound healing, repair of muscle protein, and replacement of red blood cells and antibodies. Veterinary diets will be discussed in more detail in Chapter Eleven. Here, we'll simply note that different diseases may require different nutritional strategies. While renal failure patients can generally benefit from reduced protein and phosphorus and liver disease generally means a low-protein low-fat diet, skin disease can actually be the result of low protein or a lack of fatty acids. Your veterinarian or a specialist will be your best guide in the event of illness requiring nutritional support, but Chapter Eleven will provide basic guidelines.

Less well-defined topics are how genetics may affect nutritional requirements and breed-specific nutritional considerations. Waltham notes that "digestive physiology varies with age in a breed-specific manner in dogs." Puppies of large breeds have a narrower tolerance for calcium intake than smaller breeds. Giant breeds, perhaps because of the relative dimensions of their gas-trointestinal tract and their overall size, show a higher incidence of diarrhea. Some breeds appear to have lower protein requirements, and others are prone to a copper metabolism defect.

Energy Measures— Needs and Feeds

Energy needs must be matched with energy levels in foods to achieve optimum nutrition. Therefore, both the individual dog's requirements and the actual usable energy provided by the food must be quantifiable.

Energy expenditure can be divided into resting metabolic rate, voluntary muscular activity, meal-induced thermogenesis, and adaptive thermogenesis. The *resting metabolic rate* (RMR) is the amount of energy needed to support the basic functions of respiration, circulation, and maintenance of body organs in an environment of neutral temperature (say, at room temperature) several hours following any physical activity or consumption of food. RMR accounts for 60 to 75 percent of total energy expenditure for the day. In a moderately active dog—for instance, one that jogs with the owner and plays fetch—*voluntary muscular activity* (physical exertion) may take up to 30 percent of the day's energy. After eating, *meal-induced thermogenesis* (the energy needed to digest food) uses up to 10 percent of the calories ingested.

Adaptive thermogenesis, of course, depends on the external temperature and, perhaps not so obviously, on the breed. For dogs, thermally neutral temperature (wherein they do not have to work to stay either warm or cold) falls in the range of 73 to 77°F (23 to 25°C). A study has shown that as temperatures fall, energy requirements increase more than twice as fast for Beagles as for Siberian Huskies, and even faster for Labrador Retrievers.

Now add the fact that RMR decreases with age because of the gradual loss of lean body tissue and also decreases as a result of food restriction (to the great dismay of dieters everywhere). You can start to see how complex this concept of *calories in equal calories out* can be.

Determining the amount of calories in a dog food is every bit as tricky. Chapter Five explains the concepts of gross energy, digestible energy, and metabolizable energy. Suffice to say that while it seems edifying to say that fat has more than twice the energy per unit than either proteins or carbohydrates whether or not these calories are actually used depends on whether or not the proteins, carbohydrates, and fats are provided in a form fully, partially, or nonusable by the body.

This book will attempt to answer all the questions raised here and more.

Points to Remember

- The wolf is generally classified as a carnivore, and the dog's classification is based on that. However, the tooth structure and eating habits of both indicate an omnivore that favors meat over other foods.
- Most digestion occurs in the small intestine.
- Water is absolutely essential for digestion.
- Gas (flatulence) is produced in the large intestine (important to remember in connection with bloat, a serious canine affliction that will be discussed in Chapter Eleven).
- Nutritional requirements vary throughout life span, vary with environmental conditions, and vary from dog to dog.
- Calories ingested should equal calories expended.
- The skin and coat are excellent indicators of nutritional status.

Chapter Three
The Mechanics of Feeding

Before we begin a serious discussion of *what* to feed, let's stop and take a look at *how* to feed a dog. A variety of choices must be made: what sort of bowl and other equipment to use, where your dog will eat, and perhaps when meals will occur. But the most basic of decisions is what feeding style you will use.

Free Choice, Timed, or Portion

Free Choice

The style of feeding requiring the least amount of owner participation is free choice, also known as ad libitum or self-feeding. The popularity of this method has been decreasing as dogs have moved indoors and become more accepted members of the family, but it is still used. Today, many of those who feed free choice are feeding a substantial number of dogs, in a kennel perhaps.

This method itself limits the choice of food to dry. With food left out and available to the dog at all times, anything but dry would quickly spoil or become unpalatable. Even dry food should be checked and refreshed frequently.

The main advantage usually cited for free choice—less owner involvement in feeding—may not be seen as a plus by dog owners who enjoy the satisfaction of watching their dog enjoy the food they have provided. However, other possible benefits exist.

With free choice, you do not have to determine how much to feed a dog. The dog makes the decision. Many dogs will adjust their daily intake to match their daily requirements quite accurately. Nevertheless, some will consistently overeat and quickly become obese. Free choice is *not* a good choice for such dogs. If you are beginning a free choice program, you must monitor each dog's condition to ensure that the program is working. Begin leaving food down

The dog is a social animal, and mealtime should be a family affair.

By the very act of eating many small meals, dogs keep their metabolism ticking over at a higher rate. Dogs can make their own adjustments in food intake based on amount of exercise or changes in environmental conditions if they are kept outdoors. For dogs with high energy needs, free choice may be the only way they can consume enough. For dogs who have suffered an episode of bloat, it may help prevent a recurrence.

Ad libitum feeding has two large potential drawbacks. First, some dogs simply will not adjust their intake, will consistently overeat, and thus will become obese. You must use another style of feeding for these dogs. Second, allowing dogs to feed themselves means that the owner does not observe eating habits. Refusal of food is often the first indication that a dog is ill. This can be easily missed in a self-feeding situation, and valuable time may be lost in getting the dog to a veterinarian.

Timed Feeding

The second feeding option is timed feeding. At set times each day, a large amount of food is offered to the dog, and whatever remains is picked up after a predetermined amount of time. The dog still chooses how much to eat, within the imposed time limit. Owners can observe how well their dog is eating.

With timed feeding, bowls are generally filled and put down for 15

immediately after the dogs have had their usual meal, so that they won't rush to eat everything that's offered. Give it a little time—most dogs will soon cut back on their intake to maintain an energy balance. The dogs who do not make the adjustment must be fed in a more restrained style.

In a kennel setting, feeding free choice eliminates the raucous barking that may otherwise greet feeding time. It also helps to keep kenneled dogs occupied by being able to munch many small snacks throughout the day. Subordinate dogs, who may be kept away from food bowls by more dominant individuals in a time- or portion-controlled situation, can usually eat without problem if food is available in abundant supply all the time.

to 20 minutes. Some people give only one meal a day, but nutrition experts say that feeding two meals lessens hunger and is more satisfying for the dog.

With this feeding plan, the owner can add any medications to an individual dog's bowl or even feed different foods to different dogs. Because any leftovers are picked up immediately after mealtime, the choice of dog food is not limited to dry. Any reluctance to eat will be apparent, as long as dogs in a group situation are not allowed to steal from each other.

Timed feeding is a poor choice for dogs that overeat. They will quickly learn that they have to gulp food as quickly as possible because it will be taken away from them. Such ravenous eating could increase the chance of a dog suffering bloat.

A few dogs are actually fastidious eaters and may require more than 20 minutes to eat their fill. For these dogs, timed feeding is a poor choice.

Portion Feeding

For owners with a dog or two living in their home, portion feeding is probably the most often used feeding plan. Here, the owner determines the maximum amount the dog can eat. Therefore, the owner must know how much to feed the dog.

Remember that the feeding guidelines you find on a container of food are only guidelines, on the high side of average to account for

the widest possible variation. You can use the guidelines as a starting place but will probably need to make adjustments to suit your dog. Also, if you combine foods—say, mixing canned and dry or adding fresh meats and vegetables to dog food—you need to consider *total* calories of all the foods.

In portion feeding, the dog owner decides the amount of food available to the dog.

To start, you will have to choose an amount—say, the low end of the feeding guidelines. Feed the chosen amount for a week and assess. Does your dog regularly leave food over, or seem to be gaining weight? If so, you're feeding too much. Cut back a little, try that for a week, and assess again.

If your dog scarfs up every crumb, looks to you for more, and seems to be hungry all the time, you may not be feeding enough or you may be feeding a glutton. Should your dog start to lose weight, however, you are certainly not feeding enough. Increase the amount of food, and assess again in a week or two. If

Here, a gruel for sled dogs is being mixed. House dogs don't require this much liquid in their food but often do enjoy a mixture of different foods.

Why all this variety? Well, some is frankly for price. Some is for artistic purposes. However, some is actually for the benefit of the dog. You may have noticed that the size of the dog, the length of the muzzle, and the length of the ears can all vary widely. These can affect what sort of bowl is most comfortable for a particular dog. A narrow bowl won't allow a large dog to open his mouth enough. A deep bowl could keep a short-muzzled dog from reaching the food or force the dog to plunge his whole head into the bowl.

Before you try to choose a bowl's size and shape, however, let's look at the available materials. Ceramic and stoneware bowls are generally attractive and often decorated with drawings of dogs, paw prints, or other art. Most are heavy enough not to skid readily from the action of a dog eating. They are generally shaped to be suitable for any dog, leaving you to choose only the correct size. You must consider that they are breakable. If you feed canned food, the bowl will have to be cleaned every day, and if it is dropped, it will likely break. Some also tend to be slightly porous and hard to clean thoroughly. However, many people use ceramic bowls and are quite happy with them.

Plastic bowls come in all shapes, weights, and sizes. They can be heavy, with vertical sides and a lip, or so lightweight as to blow away in a breeze. The lighter versions are often shaped into paws, dog heads,

your dog is maintaining weight nicely but putting on a starving orphan act, you need to harden your resolve and continue to feed the amount that is keeping the dog trim. Giving in will lead to obesity and all the health consequences it entails.

Bowls and Other Equipment

To feed a dog, you need a bowl. This sounds simple until you consult the latest pet supplies catalog. You can choose from stainless steel bowls, plastic bowls, ceramic bowls, and stoneware bowls. They are round, square, rectangular, or even coffin shaped. Some are deep with slanted sides, others are shallow with vertical sides.

Some have two or more compartments, and some even grow taller along with your dog.

or two compartments side by side. Most are small, but even a small dog can push these nearly weightless plastics around. The heavier versions are preferable. They will stand up to rough handling by the dog owner but not as much from the dog. Teeth can inflict some serious damage on these bowls, even tear them into shreds. If mealtime is supervised and bowls are taken away at other times, this problem can be avoided. Plastic bowls clean well but can crack if left in cold weather or melt enough to deform in hot weather. Scratches and cracks can become breeding grounds for bacteria.

Metal bowls also come in a variety of weights. The heavier, non-seam, stainless steel bowls are excellent choices. They are impervious to weather, dog teeth, cleaning, and rough handling. Some even come with decorations stamped into the rim for those who like their bowls to be pretty. They should not be used as water bowls outdoors in cold weather. Drinking out of them in such conditions could be akin to licking a flagpole in below-freezing temperatures.

Whatever material you prefer, it should fit these guidelines:
- Easy to clean thoroughly
- Capable of withstanding some rough handling by both owner and dog
- Nontoxic (including any decorations) and nonreactive with all the substances in dog food
- Resistant to cracking or breaking

Once you have chosen a material, you need to consider shape and size. Basically, the bowl should be big enough to hold the dog's ration of food and allow the dog to open its mouth comfortably. There are one or two other special considerations.

For dogs like Basset Hounds, Afghan Hounds, and Cocker Spaniels, keeping those long, floppy ears out of each day's dinner can be a challenge. Some owners use a snood. This cylindrical piece of cloth slides over the dog's head and corrals those ears. You can also choose a bowl designed to help. These are deeper and narrower, oval or even coffin shaped with the pointed end meant to be positioned in a corner so the dog can't push the bowl around. Just be sure the bowl is wide enough for the dog's face and narrow enough to keep the ears out of the bowl on either side.

Puppies also benefit from special bowls or, more accurately, pans. Those little uncoordinated bodies do better with low, wide pans. You can even buy something called the

Bowls come in a wide variety of materials, shapes, and sizes.

flying saucer puppy feeding dish. Low on the outside, it has a flared cone sticking up in the middle, sloping out to the edge. This keeps food out toward the edge of the dish and discourages puppies from lying or walking in the food.

Those owners choosing an ad libitum style can purchase self-feeders. These are large bins into which you can pour dry food. They have an opening at the bottom, allowing the dog to stick his or her head in and munch a few mouthfuls whenever the mood may strike.

Whatever type of bowl you choose to use for your dog's food and water, you must be committed to keeping it clean. Water bowls should be free of algae and scum. Dog food bowls should be scrubbed every day if you are using canned food and at least wiped out if you are using dry food.

If your dog eats outside, your supervision will ensure that your dog, rather than birds or wild animals, actually eats the food. (Also, your dog will be much happier if you are there when he eats—you are his pack, after all.) Any leftovers can attract animals if they are not picked up.

For the dog that lives outside . . . first, why isn't your dog inside, sharing life with the family? Whatever reasons you may have for keeping a dog outdoors, you must take some extra precautions. Water should never be allowed to freeze. Special heated bowls are available (or you could just bring the dog inside). In the summer, water should be kept in the shade (and remember that shade moves throughout the day). You could even get a special bowl with a compartment under it to fill with ice. Some food bowls have moats around them to keep insects from crawling into the food. (However, wouldn't it be easier just to welcome the dog into your home?!)

Other Equipment and Considerations

For larger dogs, you might consider providing a feeding platform of some sort. A dog eats by snatching a mouthful of food and with a quick toss of the head, flinging the food back onto the tongue. It's then rolled back down the tongue and swallowed. This process is made more difficult if the dog is bending to the ground like a giraffe. The dog may even swallow more air and increase the risk of suffering an episode of bloat (to be discussed in Chapter Eleven).

A variety of raised feeders can be purchased. Wire racks generally hold both food and water dishes and come in several heights. Molded plastic offers several options. One is a sort of tabletop on four legs, with cutouts to hold two stainless bowls. It's sturdy and attractive, but comes in only two heights. Another is extravagantly adjustable, from less than a foot to nearly two feet high. It can grow as the dog grows. At its lower setting, this feeder looks like a plain cylinder with a bowl set in the top. But as you pull it up, a corrugated construction becomes obvious. Finally, a third design uses a column based in a round, weighted foot. Holders for stainless bowls stick out on either side and can ride up and down the column to adjust their height.

A self-feeder dispenses a constant supply of dry food so the dog can eat at will.

Of course, you could always make your own feeding platform. Even a wooden crate could serve the purpose if it is the correct height and positioned so that the bowl cannot be pushed off of it. Or if you are a passable carpenter, you could construct a box to hold a bowl at the correct height and provide some storage underneath, perhaps for a bag or some cans of food.

Finally, where should your dog eat? Dogs are creatures of habit and will appreciate a set place where their food is provided. Many owners choose the kitchen for its ease in cleaning up any spills. As long as the dog can stand comfortably on the floor, that's an acceptable choice. If you do use a feeding platform, it will probably remain in position, serving as the dog's dinner table. Wherever you feed the dog, he or she will be happiest if you are within view. Dogs are communal eaters. They will also know their dinnertime and remind you if you are late with the chow, as any dog owner will attest.

Dogs may appreciate an elevated feeding platform. These homemade versions offer the advantage of catching spills and providing storage space.

Points to Remember

- Free choice is an appropriate choice as long as the dog will restrict its food intake to what is needed for maintenance.
- Timed feeding can teach dogs to bolt food in order to get as much as possible before the food is picked up.
- Portion feeding puts the responsibility for determining the amount of food on the owner.
- Bowls should be easy to clean, relatively nonbreakable, nontoxic,

resistant to cracking, and sized for the dog.
- Dogs with long ears, dogs with short snouts, and puppies all benefit from different types of bowls.
- Water should be provided at all times and should never be allowed to freeze or sit in the sun all day.
- Bowls must be kept clean.
- Large dogs may benefit from eating off a raised platform.
- Dogs will appreciate their own regular place to eat and a regular feeding time.

Chapter Four

So How Do You Choose?

To introduce you to the information in upcoming chapters and start you thinking about how to choose a dog food, we will now look at *almost twenty questions*. You will not yet have the answers to many of them but will have a framework for your thoughts as you continue through the book.

Considerations Before Choosing a Dog Food

1. Are you going to use commercial food or a homemade diet?

If you decide to use a homemade diet, you must be careful to provide good nutrition and safe ingredients. You will need to be particularly careful to introduce the diet gradually. You cannot decide you're too tired to bother and serve your dog leftover spaghetti one night and French toast the next. You will need a tested recipe and all the unusual ingredients it calls for. (You can find more about homemade diets in Chapter Eleven.)

2. Do you plan to feed free choice or by timed or portioned meals?

If you plan to feed free choice, skip the next question—your only option will be dry food. Remember to pay careful attention to your dog's weight and general health. Continue feeding free choice only if the dog maintains a healthy weight.

If your dog tends toward gluttony, portion feeding is your best choice. Feeding two meals a day rather than one will help keep the dog's metabolism ticking and help the dog feel more full. You will take the responsibility for determining the calories your dog ingests.

Timed feeding can encourage bolting of food and is usually not the best choice.

3. Do you want to use dry, semi-moist, canned, or refrigerated food or some mixture of these?

You may not yet be ready to answer this, but here are some pros and cons of each.

Dry food is economical, can be bought in bulk, and is easy to store. It may be fed free choice. It requires

higher in meat and protein content than other forms, energy dense, and highly palatable. They do not require preservatives but do require appropriate storage.

Any type can be mixed with any other type or with some homemade ingredients (as long as the homemade portion is a small enough percentage not to throw off the vitamin and mineral proportions of the commercial food). One study has suggested that mixing canned and dry may actually improve overall digestion. Dog owners may enjoy the extra feeling of involvement from mixing types of food.

preservatives to prevent rancidity. It comes in different sizes, shapes, and flavors. It is highly processed.

Canned food is highly palatable and comes in a wide variety of flavors. It may be formed as a meatloaf or a stew. Cans are easy to store until opened and then must be refrigerated. No preservatives are required, though some canned foods do include them.

Semimoist food, packaged into burgers or chunks, is neat and easy to feed. Its palatability is generally high but so is the level of preservatives, humectants (to keep the product moist), and artificial colors and flavors. It is easy to store, and small, individually portioned packages are generally used when opened.

Refrigerated/frozen foods generally come either in plastic-encased rolls or in small one- to two-portion boxes. These foods are usually

4. What about table scraps? Can they be added to food or given as a treat?

Table scraps are all right as long as they are kept to no more than 5 percent of the daily calories. Do not just think meat—dogs may enjoy vegetables, grains, fruits, almost anything you yourself would eat. However, definitely avoid small, splintery bones and chocolate. (Read Chapter Six for more about table scraps and treats.)

5. Is your dog in a life stage that might require a special diet? (A complete discussion can be found in Chapter Nine.)

Puppies need higher levels of energy to fuel growth, but evidence now shows that the fastest growth rate is not the healthiest. Special large-breed puppy foods have been developed for those that will weigh

60 pounds or more as adults. These foods (as well as a few regular puppy foods) are lower in protein and calcium than the average puppy food. Excess calcium in any puppy diet (or from unwise supplementation) contributes to skeletal disorders.

Reproducing bitches require increasing nutrition from the fifth week of pregnancy through the fourth week of lactation. The increasing burden of puppies makes it physically difficult for the bitch to consume large quantities of food in one meal. However, inadequate diet during reproduction can have serious detrimental consequences for the bitch and her puppies. Bitches will need as many as five or six meals a day to get enough food.

Senior dogs may continue to thrive on a regular adult dog food or may benefit from the decreased salt and protein of a senior diet. No legal definition of *senior* or *geriatric* diets exists, so check ingredients and guaranteed analyses carefully. Some think that older dogs (just like older people) may benefit from supplementation with antioxidants and enzymes. Many older dogs become underweight, so monitor their condition carefully.

Hard-working dogs—sled dogs, hunting dogs during field trial or hunting season, herding dogs that practice their craft daily—may need a *performance* diet higher in fat and calories. The roll type, high-meat foods may be a good choice. The timing of meals is also crucial—small snacks throughout the work-ing day may help keep the dog in good working order.

6. Does your dog have any medical conditions that might require special dietary consideration?

Some genetic abnormalities—such as copper storage disease, hyperlipidemia, and zinc deficiency—and some diseases—for example, liver disease, colitis, and diabetes—can benefit from specific dietary adjustments. Veterinary diets are available through veterinarians and should be used only per their advice. (You can learn more about veterinary diets in Chapter Eleven.)

7. Do you have any special expectations of a dog food, say, a vegetarian diet or an all-natural formulation?

Vegetarian diets are available for dogs. They will probably provide adequate nutrition for adult dogs but are not appropriate for puppies or reproducing bitches. Most vegetarian formulations include soy, which may present a problem for some dogs.

The term *natural* has no legal definition when applied to dog food as yet. In general, though, it is taken to mean the absence of artificial flavors, colors, and preservatives. Commercial diets meeting these specifications are available.

People who define a natural diet as a whole, raw-foods diet will have to formulate their own food. They must be careful to handle raw meats safely and to provide balanced nutrition.

At dog shows, you will usually find vendor booths selling dog food as well as other dog-related items.

Avoid jumping into the latest fad—it may be unproven, even dangerous. Some people do try to turn a quick buck by providing a fad food without regard for the consequences. (See Chapter Eleven for a more complete discussion of these issues.)

8. Is your dog overweight?

Be honest. Use the Body Condition Scoring text and illustration from Chapter Ten to assess your dog's trimness. If your dog is only slightly chubby, simply cutting out treats or cutting back on food and increasing exercise should be sufficient to correct the problem. Do not feed a chubby dog free choice.

If your dog is more seriously overweight, a reduced-calorie food may be in order. The designation *light* is now more tightly regulated, so these foods really are lower in calories. Many have higher levels of fiber and may cause digestive disturbances in some dogs.

Obesity can have severe health consequences, including heart disease, a tendency to diabetes, impaired liver function, breathing impairment, increased stress on joints, impaired reproductive capabilities, and potential anesthesia and surgery complications.

9. Do you and your veterinarian suspect that your dog has food allergies or a food intolerance?

Remember, food intolerance will cause symptoms the first time the dog eats the particular food, resulting in diarrhea or vomiting. Food allergies take a couple of years to develop and will manifest themselves as itchy skin. Proteins are the most common allergens, with beef and soy topping the list. However, flea allergies are far more common than food allergies, so be sure to check out that possibility first.

The only absolute way to determine food allergies is through an elimination diet, fed under the supervision of your veterinarian. (For more about allergies, read Chapter Eleven.)

So, now you know if you are going to choose any sort of special diet and perhaps if you will be using a dry, canned, semimoist, or refrigerated food or some mixture of these. How do you go about choosing the one particular brand and flavor from the hundreds available? You will need to examine some of your beliefs and what is important to you.

10. Do you think the dog is a carnivore or an omnivore?

If you still believe the dog is a carnivore, you will be happier with the high meat content of the refrigerated roll type products if you haven't already decided to use a raw-meats homemade diet. These roll type products are available through fewer outlets than other forms of food but can often be found at dog shows or mail ordered.

If you believe the dog is an omnivore, this will not be a major issue.

11. Do you believe a dog food should contain much the same ingredients we ourselves eat?

If you feel that chicken contains better nutrition than chicken meal, or cottage cheese than dried whey products, consult the list of ingredients on the dog foods. Some ingredients could appear on labels of foods for human consumption without causing a raised eyebrow. Chapter Seven discusses ingredients, and many of those unfamiliar names found in ingredients lists are defined in the glossary.

12. A related question—do you feel that less-processed ingredients offer better nutrition than more-processed ones?

We're back to chicken versus chicken meal or corn versus corn gluten meal. Meals can actually be more nutrient dense, though not necessarily so. But if you feel something is lost in the processing, you will be happier with more whole-food ingredients.

13. Do you feel that processing of the product as a whole is a problem?

All commercial diets are cooked somehow. Most dry foods are extruded, but some are baked. Foods in the form of flakes or randomly sized, uneven kibbles are probably baked.

Semimoist foods are probably the most processed of all. Canned foods are held at temperatures of approximately 250 degrees for an hour or more. Roll type products are baked.

14. Do you know what information can be found on dog food packages and where to find it?

The package label is actually designed to satisfy legal requirements. However, some information can be useful in your quest for a dog food. The statement, "Animal feeding tests using AAFCO procedures have been conducted," means that the food has been fed to dogs with good results. Even though critics claim the test period is too short, it is better than no test period at all.

Ingredients are listed in descending order by weight. Keep in mind that some may be dry weights and some water-added weights and that some may be listed more than once under different names—corn, ground corn, and corn gluten meal, for example. No reference to quality of ingredients is permitted on packaging, and the ingredients list is not necessarily an indication of quality.

The guaranteed analysis is only a rough indication of nutritional value at best, but can let you compare relative levels of protein and fat between foods.

Product freshness dating is one of the most important pieces of information to be found on the label and should always be checked. The manufacturer's toll-free number (or mailing address) will let you contact the manufacturer and ask any questions you may have. (For a more complete discussion of product labels and feeding trials, see Chapter Eight.)

15. Do you have concerns about preservatives?

With a recent FDA request for lowered levels of ethoxyquin in pet foods, concern may be justified. Many manufacturers have shifted away from artificial preservatives such as ethoxyquin, BHA, and BHT in favor of vitamin E and mixed tocopherols. Keep in mind that these more natural substances are also less powerful and will not protect against oxidation and rancidity for as long. You may want to not only check product freshness dating but call and ask the manufacturer how long they consider their preservatives effective. Some claim natural preservatives are good for up to three months but others say no more than 30 days. (Chapter Seven examines the preservative issue.)

16. Do you prefer an old company or a new company?

Do you believe that a company that has been in business for many years has proven by its continued existence that it offers a quality product? Or do you believe that new companies offer new ideas, innovation, and more up-to-date thinking and technology?

If the former line of thought makes sense to you, you will be comfortable with one of the dog food manufacturers on the scene for 30 years or more. If you find the latter premise appealing, you may want to choose one of the newer companies on the pet food scene. There are plenty of those as well. Show a little healthy skepticism regarding overblown claims of being the "healthiest dog food ever" or "the only all-natural" food.

17. Which nutritional considerations do you consider most important?

After reading Chapter Five about nutrition, you will know that the basic needs a food must supply are:
- Sufficient energy for the metabolism of the food, thermal regulation, and daily activity
- All of the essential amino acids
- Fat for energy, brain chemistry, and absorption of the fat-soluble vitamins
- Protein for maintenance of cellular structures
- Water-soluble vitamins C and the B complex, which can't be stored in the body
- Both omega-3 and omega-6 essential fatty acids
- The 22 minerals required by the dog, in correct proportions
Additional considerations are:
- Carbohydrates, which can supply energy and leave proteins to perform cell-building activities

- Fiber to play a role in gastrointestinal health, preferably of moderate fermentability and low solubility
- Antioxidants to counteract the action of free radicals
- Enzymes to promote digestion

Assessing Your Dog Food Choice

Keep these *almost twenty questions* in mind as you read the rest of the book, and you will have a good idea of what you are going to look for when choosing a dog food. If you are still uncertain, consult your veterinarian or dog-owning friends. Ask for recommendations.

However, your job is not over once you have chosen a food. To know that you have made a good choice, you must assess the food's performance. In fact, you should continue to assess your dog's nutrition throughout his or her life.

Does your dog eat the chosen food readily? A food cannot provide nutrition if it isn't eaten. Take your dog's acceptance of change into account—if he turns his nose up at every new treat, don't condemn a food because he doesn't chow down right away. Mix a small amount of the new food thoroughly into the old food. Gradually increase the amount and see if your dog will grow to love it.

Keep an eye on your dog's waistline. Different foods have different caloric densities. You don't want extra pounds creeping up on your pooch. You also want to be sure you're sup-

plying *enough* calories. Feeding the proper amount of a quality food throughout a dog's life definitely contributes to good health and longevity.

Unappetizing as the prospect may be, it pays to keep an eye on your dog's stool. It should be well formed but not hard and compacted. The quantity will depend to some extent on your philosophy in choosing a food—if you believe a diet should have fiber to clean out the intestines, the quantity of stool will be greater than if you believe in a high-meat diet.

Finally, the condition of your dog's haircoat is an excellent indication of good or bad nutrition. Hair is composed mainly of protein. In order for the hair to shine with health, the food must satisfy the basic needs of metabolism, thermogenesis, and energy and have enough nutrition left to supply luster to the haircoat. A dull coat could mean a lot of things, but one of the possibilities is poor nutrition.

A good coat requires good nutrition.

Chapter Five

Nutrition

The subject of canine nutrition is every bit as confusing and constantly changing as the subject of human nutrition. Pet food manufacturers keep large staffs of scientists and nutritionists and kennels full of dogs to develop and test new food formulations. The big difference is that while humans may eat two dozen different foods a day, dogs are generally fed one food and one food only.

For that reason, dog food alone, with the addition only of water, must maintain the dog in optimum health. "A proper diet is key to enhancing a pet's opportunity to remain healthy. By introducing good nutrition early in a puppy's life you can add to the overall health and well being of your pet," says Dr. James Sokolowski, DVM, Ph.D., professional services manager at Waltham USA. That means quality proteins for growth, muscle tone, and constant repair of body tissues; fats for high energy, glossy coats, and absorption of fat-soluble vitamins; carbohydrates for energy and a healthy digestive tract; vitamins for efficient metabolism; minerals and trace elements for strong teeth and bones. The illustra-

tion on the next page pictures these essential nutrients in the relative quantities in which they are required.

A *complete* food contains all of the required nutrients. A *complete and balanced* food contains all of the required nutrients in the proper proportions. (In Chapter Eleven we will investigate the contentions of some critics of commercial dog food that there is no such thing as one complete and balanced food.)

Alphabet Soup

Just as with people, pet nutritionists determine the minimum daily requirement (MDR) for each nutrient. This is the minimum that must be provided each day for proper metabolic processes to occur. However, these minimums change with variations in size, activity level, life stage, and even breed. To cover a wider range of normal, healthy individuals, dog food manufacturers adjust the MDR upward based on experience and feeding trials to derive the recommended daily allowance (RDA).

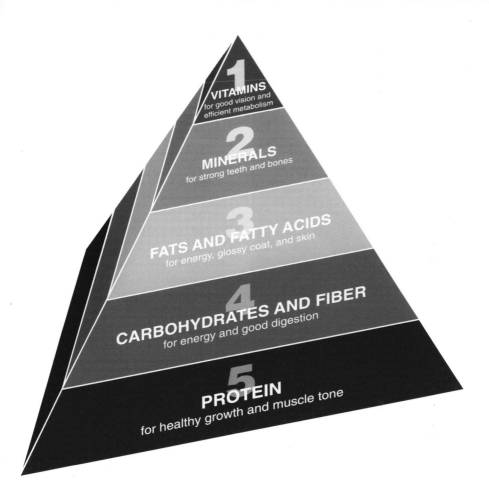

1 **VITAMINS**
for good vision and
efficient metabolism

2 **MINERALS**
for strong teeth and bones

3 **FATS AND FATTY ACIDS**
for energy, glossy coat, and skin

4 **CARBOHYDRATES AND FIBER**
for energy and good digestion

5 **PROTEIN**
for healthy growth and muscle tone

The RDA should provide adequate amounts of all the necessary nutrients for a broad spectrum of the canine population. However, even the RDA is only a guideline. As we have already noted, the true measure of how much of a complete and balanced food your dog should consume each day is energy. The energy in a food is determined by the amounts and kinds of fats, proteins, and carbohydrates. Consuming more energy than is required means that the excess energy will be stored as body fat. The amount of energy in the daily diet must be close to actual requirements to keep an animal healthy, lively, and trim.

Energy is expressed in kilocalories (kcal or sometimes C, as in Calorie with a capital C). In the body, energy is derived by oxidizing (*burning*) food in a series of enzyme-

Active dogs will burn more calories.

closer to the food actually digested and absorbed. However, some of this will be only partially available to the body's tissues, and some will be lost in the urine.

Metabolizable energy (ME) takes the DE and subtracts the GE of the urine. This figure is as close as we can get to the energy actually utilized by the animal's tissues.

Animals, whether canine or human, can have wide variations in the efficiency of their metabolisms. Through feeding trials with hundreds of dogs, manufacturers were able to develop a formula to give the approximate ME of a food based on its content of proteins, fats, and carbohydrates. Once they could calculate the ME of a food, manufacturers could give reasonable feeding guidelines if they knew the energy requirements of dogs.

Energy use has two main components. Resting metabolic rate (RMR), as we've already seen, is the *resting* energy, the energy needed to support respiration, circulation, and function of the body's organs. RMR changes slowly in relation to age, weight, and hormonal shifts.

Thermogenesis (both adaptive and meal-induced) is the energy used for movement, digesting and utilizing nutrients, and maintaining body temperature. Thermogenesis needs can change rapidly in relation to environmental conditions and the health of the animal.

Energy requirements are generally measured in relation to heat

regulated chemical reactions. Any nutrients not digested are eliminated as urine or feces. Because the potential energy in nutrients is not totally digestible, energy intake is considered at three levels.

Gross energy (GE) is all the energy released by complete oxidation of the food. This is determined by burning the food in pure oxygen in a machine that can measure the heat released in the process. Obviously, this does not reflect what actually happens when an animal eats a food.

Digestible energy (DE) is closer to reality. It takes the GE of the whole food and subtracts the GE of the feces to arrive at a measure

loss or production. The leading dog food manufacturers use metabolic body size (MBS, roughly body surface area) in calculating feeding guidelines because heat loss varies in relation to surface area, not weight. However, they express their feeding guidelines in kcal ME per pound of body weight.

When energy input matches energy output, an animal is in energy balance. Even a very small imbalance, over time, can result in weight gain or loss. In general, energy requirements per pound of body weight decrease as the size of the dog increases. That is, a toy dog weighing 11 pounds will require roughly 40 kcal of energy per pound of body weight. A 20-pound dog will need 34 kcal per pound. A dog weighing 55 pounds will be down to 27 kcal per pound. These are, of course, just guidelines.

The Essential Nutrients

A living body requires nutrients. Consuming food is the body's way of gaining nutrients. Just how much is gained depends on what is consumed and how digestible it is. Each nutrient is important in itself and in relation to other nutrients. Dogs and humans are both omnivores and can gain their nutrients from a wide variety of sources, both plant and animal. Any animal's nutritional health depends on receiving the correct amounts and propor-

tions of water, proteins, fats, carbohydrates, vitamins, and minerals.

Proteins

Proteins can come from both plants and animals. They are critical to the diet, being the primary components of muscle, bone, blood, and immune system agents. Protein (or, to be more correct, the amino acids that compose protein) is vital to growth, development, repair of tissues, sexual development, hormone production, metabolism, function of the nervous and immune systems, and formation of DNA.

There are 22 amino acids. Ten of them are considered essential because a dog can't synthesize enough of them internally and they must be supplied in the food. Different foods provide different balances of the amino acids. While beef is very high in lysine (one of the essential amino acids), corn is deficient in it. However, a combination of corn and soy provides all of the essential amino acids. Only whole eggs and

Protein is essential for good growth, and these lively Samoyed puppies have plenty of growing to do.

Lamb and rice dog foods have become increasingly popular.

chemical score. Eggs have a chemical value of 100. Fish is rated in the low 90s. Beef falls in the high 70s. Wheat scores 60, but wheat gluten only 40. Corn rates in the mid-50s. Pet food manufacturers combine a variety of protein (amino acid) sources to increase the overall chemical score of the finished food. Adding a protein source low in only valine to a source deficient in lysine but high in valine can result in a combined chemical score of 100.

milk contain all of the essential amino acids within themselves.

The essential amino acids are

Phenylalanine

Valine

Threonine

Tryptophan

Isoleucine

Methionine

Histidine

Arginine

Leucine

Lysine

These amino acids give a protein its *chemical score* (also called biological score). Comparing the amounts of essential amino acids in a protein source with the requirements established for an animal in a particular life stage results in a percentage. If all of the essential amino acid requirements are met, the protein's chemical score is 100. If the protein supplies 100 percent of some essential amino acids but only 60 percent of another, the chemical score is 60. The essential amino acid in the shortest supply is defined as the "first limiting amino acid." Its percentage is used as the

However, chemical scores are not listed on dog food packaging (or, for that matter, on foods for human consumption). Foods that have passed AAFCO feeding trials almost certainly contain 100 percent of the essential amino acids.

The most common meat sources of protein are beef, chicken, turkey, and lamb. Other animal sources include meat by-products, eggs, milk, whey, and cheese. The most common plant sources are wheat, corn, rice, soy, and barley. Both plant and animal proteins can provide good nutrition, and a high-quality plant source is preferable over a low-quality animal source.

Quality control during food processing is extremely important, because proteins and vitamins can be damaged by excessive heat. Vegetable sources, in particular, must be carefully processed if they are to be of use to the dog, whose enzyme system is not geared toward a vegetarian diet.

Enzymes are related to proteins, consisting of a protein molecule

Sources of Carbohydrates in Dog Foods Include

Cereal Grains	Milling Products	Milk Products
Corn	Corn gluten meal	Dried skim milk
Oats	Oatmeal	Dried whey
Wheat	Wheat middlings	
Rice	Rice hulls	
Barley	Beet pulp	

and a *coenzyme* (a nonprotein chemical derivative of a vitamin). Enzymes can be classified into four basic groups: *amylases*, which break down carbohydrates; *lipases*, which break down fats; *proteases*, which break down proteins; and *cellulases*, which break down vegetable matter, including fiber. Enzyme action is required to degrade food substances and make the nutrients available to the body. David Dzanis, veterinary nutritionist with the FDA's Center for Veterinary Medicine, notes, "Dogs don't have cellulase, except for some minor activity in the lower gut." So they are at a disadvantage when digesting vegetable matter.

The protein in an adult food, whatever its source, usually supplies 20 to 25 percent of total calories. High-fat foods, because of nutritional interrelationships, require higher levels of protein, up to 30 percent.

Carbohydrates

Dogs actually have no minimum daily requirements for carbohydrates because extra protein can provide the necessary nutrients. However, most dog foods do include carbohydrates for taste, added energy, and fiber for digestive health. (Dry foods, in fact, require carbohydrates in their formulations to permit the extrusion process to operate.) Carbohydrates come mainly from plant sources. The digestible carbohydrate portion of the plant (also referred to as *nitrogen-free extract* or *NFE*) is in the form of simple sugars such as glucose and larger molecules such as starch, which consists of chains of simpler sugars. Carbohydrates supply energy, particularly quick energy. Without sufficient supplies, the body will turn to its own tissues for fuel. Too high an energy supply will mean that glycogen is stored as body fat.

Grains and other starches provide energy, B complex vitamins, and fiber.

Fermentability and Solubility of Fiber Sources

Fiber	Solubility	Fermentability
Beet pulp	Low	Moderate
Cellulose	Low	Low
Rice bran	Low	Moderate
Gum arabic	High	Moderate
Pectin	Low	High
C-M cellulose	High	Low
Methylcellulose	High	Low
Cabbage fiber	Low	High
Guar gum	High	High
Locust bean gum	High	Low
Xanthan gum	High	Moderate

From Iams. June 1994. Advances in Fiber Nutrition. *Topics in Practical Nutrition*. Vol. 4, No. 2. Used with permission.

Carbohydrates are protein sparing. They provide a source of energy and good maintenance of blood glucose levels. Diets containing carbohydrates result in a higher rate of glucose utilization than carbohydrate-free diets.

Starch-containing cereal grains and legumes must be processed by grinding or flaking and then thoroughly cooked to allow for optimum digestion. If fed raw, they often produce diarrhea.

The nondigestible portions of plants, composed of cell walls, cellulose, and lignin, are called *crude fiber*. Most of the fiber traditionally found in dog foods was cellulose or compounds similar to cellulose. However, research now indicates that fiber in dog foods should not just provide bulk but facilitate pro-

duction of short-chain fatty acids (SCFAs). These SCFAs provide energy to the intestinal walls, helping them to renew tissues and maintain gastrointestinal health. Cellulose does not perform this function, but other fibers, such as beet pulp and rice bran, do. Good fiber sources have moderate fermentability and low solubility. As you can see by the table, beet pulp and rice bran have the correct solubility and fermentability.

A high content of insoluble, nonfermentable fiber such as cellulose means that food passes rapidly through the dog's digestive system. This rapid passage means that food is not exposed to the digestive enzymes for sufficient time, and digestion efficiency suffers. As the amount of nonfermentable fiber increases, protein digestibility, energy digestibility, fat digestibility, dry matter digestibility, and selective mineral absorption decreases. The frequency and volume of bowel movements both increase. Too much fermentability can result in loose stools. Too much solubility can mean hard, compacted stools.

Use of fiber has been advocated to treat constipation, obesity, and inflammatory bowel disease. However, we now see that the *quality* of fiber is at least as important as the *quantity*. Different analyses of dog food will result in differing levels of fiber. So foods may have a lot more fiber than is listed on the label.

Fats

Fats supply roughly twice the energy per gram as do proteins and carbohydrates (8.5 kcal compared with 3.5 kcal). Fats are necessary for the absorption of the fat-soluble vitamins, which are critical to overall cell health. Much of a food's texture and palatability comes from fat. However, as you've probably heard, fat is high in calories. Where a pound of corn (itself not regarded as a slimming food) contains 1,585 calories, a pound of animal fat contains a whopping 4,100 calories. So dogs must eat less of a high-fat diet if they are to avoid having dietary fat end up as body fat.

Fat is an extremely efficient nutrient, with more than 90 percent digestibility. It can be stored in the body without appreciable amounts of water or minerals. High-fat diets have a high potential for upsetting the balance of total nutrient intake and creating nutrient deficiencies.

Fats are composed of triglycerides. Each triglyceride is a combination of three fatty acids. These fatty acids are crucial to skin and haircoat health, and are components of cell walls. Three *essential fatty acids*—linoleic, alpha-linolenic, and arachidonic acids—must be either supplied in the diet or converted from some other nutrient.

Linoleic acid has long been considered a dietary essential. Deficiencies result in problems seen in the haircoat, the paw pads, and the surface of the nose. The dog (but not the cat) can convert linoleic to both alpha-linolenic and arachidonic fatty acids, thus accounting for the three traditional essential fatty acids.

Signs of a diet deficient in fat or the right kinds of fatty acids include a dull haircoat, dry flaking skin, signs of fat-soluble vitamin deficiency, and poor growth in puppies. Essential fatty acids are easily destroyed by heat, light, and oxygen. The processing involved in the manufacture of dog foods must be carefully regulated to avoid destruction of these nutrients. Rancidity must also be prevented.

Look for a food that provides the beneficial fatty acids. Fish oils, beef, pork, and unprocessed oil seeds such as flax and sesame are all good sources. Remember that several weeks will pass before the benefits of the better food will take effect.

Vitamins

Vitamins maintain a balance between constructive and destructive cellular changes and help the body to resist disease. They fall into two categories: fat soluble (A, D, E, and K) and water soluble (the B complex and C). All of them must be carefully balanced to avoid excesses, deficiencies, or interference with one another.

The fat-soluble vitamins can be stored in the tissues, primarily in body fat and in the liver. Most dogs (though not young puppies) have a reserve to draw on if necessary. Because they can be stored, toxicity is a risk if dietary levels of fat-soluble vitamins are too high.

Vitamin A (retinol) is essential for growth of bones, good maintenance of the skin, proper functioning of the kidneys, and vision in dim light. In nature, it exists in the form of a precursor, the carotenoids. These are the yellow or orange pigments in fruits and vegetables, beta-carotene being the most well-known and most biologically available. The carotenoids can be transformed into vitamin A in the body.

Vitamin D is critical in the process that allows the body to use calcium and phosphorus to develop teeth and bones. After undergoing a series of chemical conversions in the liver and kidneys, it works to raise blood levels of calcium and phosphorus to those required for mineralization of bone.

Vitamin E (tocopherols) is widely distributed among green plants, vegetable oils, nuts, legumes, and wheat germ. It serves as an antioxidant, protecting cell membranes from damage as well as shielding vitamin A and carotene from oxidation. However, vitamin E itself is subject to destruction by oxidation, particularly if fats in the food become rancid. The mixed tocopherols used as a natural preservative in foods are not generally high in bioavailability and should not be counted in the diet's level of vitamin E.

Vitamin K is actually a group of seven quinone derivatives, essential for blood coagulation and clotting. Dogs can synthesize vitamin K in their intestines.

There are even more water-soluble vitamins. They are washed out of the body each day and must be constantly replaced. The B complex vitamins are used to form coenzymes necessary in biochemical reactions, utilization of food, and production of energy. Natural sources of B vitamins, such as yeast, liver, meat, poultry, rice, and wheat germ, are preferred over synthetic preparations.

Thiamine (B1 or aneurine) is obtained from natural foodstuffs through bacterial synthesis. It acts as a coenzyme in the metabolism of carbohydrates. Hard-working dogs consuming more carbohydrates require higher levels of thiamine. Thiamine is progressively destroyed by cooking and also by thiaminase, found in raw fish and some plants. Manufacturers normally add large quantities of thiamine before processing so that even after losses the finished product will meet or exceed recommendations. Thiamine has low toxicity, so extra amounts are not a problem.

Riboflavin (B2) is involved in several enzyme systems important in carbohydrate and amino acid metabolism. It is required for normal growth. The requirement for riboflavin is strongly influenced by environmental temperature, with more required as temperatures drop. This is another vitamin that manufacturers supply in large quantities to avoid deficiencies. Symptoms of such deficiencies would include weight loss, eye lesions, and dry flaky skin.

Niacin is actually a generic name for two separate compounds, nicotinamide and nicotinic acid. Both are required as components of coenzymes needed for utilization of all major nutrients. Diets in which corn is a major ingredient can create deficiencies because the nicotinic acid in cereals is in bound form, not a biochemically available form.

Pyridoxine (B6) can be supplied by fish, liver, milk, soy, wheat germ, or yeast. It is actually three related compounds: pyridoxine, pyridoxal, and pyridoxamine. Any one of these can be converted to any of the others. They are involved in the metabolism of proteins and fats.

Pantothenic acid is a component of coenyzme A, which is essential in metabolizing all the major nutrients. Deficiencies are unlikely because pantothenic acid is widely available from both animal and plant tissues.

Biotin functions as a coenzyme necessary for carbon dioxide fixation. It is present in yeast, peanuts, molasses, organ meats, milk, egg yolks, and legumes. However, in the body, it is primarily synthesized by bacteria in the digestive system. Biotin deficiency occurs only when biotin's action is suppressed by antibiotics or when large measures of raw egg white are included in the diet. The glycoprotein *avidin* found in egg whites binds with biotin and renders it biologically unavailable. Cooking destroys avidin.

Folic acid (folacin or folate) is found in organ meats, green leafy vegetables, yeast, soy, and alfalfa meal. It is necessary for reproduction, formation of red blood cells, and synthesis of thymidine, an essential component of DNA.

Choline is a component of phospholipids (essential components of cell membranes) and a precursor of acetylcholine (a neurotransmitter

Dogs receiving the correct balance of vitamins and other nutrients should be active and energetic.

41

Symptoms of Vitamin Deficiencies and Excesses

Vitamin	Deficiency	Excess
A	Eye dryness Corneal ulcers Conjunctivitis Night blindness Skin lesions Loss of appetite/weight Staggering walk	Crippling bone disease Tooth loss Severe liver damage (All usually a result of too much fish oil or liver in the diet, seen more in cats than dogs)
D	Rickets Osteomalacia	Deformed teeth and jaws Calcification of soft tissues Graying of dark hair
E	Reproductive failure Degeneration of muscles Immune system impairment	
B1	Anorexia Constipation Weight loss Tonic convulsions Heart failure	
B2	Weight loss Eye lesions Dry, flaky skin	
Niacin	Darkening of the tongue Inflammation of the mouth Foul breath Thick drool, often blood stained	
Pyridoxine	Anemia Anorexia Loss of mental function Convulsions	
Pantothenic acid	Unlikely	
Biotin	Unlikely	
Folic acid	Unlikely	
Choline	Unlikely	
B12	Pernicious anemia Degeneration of mental function Depressed growth	

chemical involved in transmission of nerve impulses). Choline deficiency creates liver and kidney dysfunction; but choline is widely available and its function can even be taken over by methionine, so deficiency is highly unlikely.

Vitamin B12 is the only vitamin that contains a trace element (cobalt). Its coenzyme is needed for synthesis of DNA. It is involved in fat and carbohydrate metabolism and synthesis of nerve tissue called myelin.

Vitamin C (ascorbic acid) can be synthesized from glucose by most mammals, so no dietary requirement exists. (Interestingly, the primates, including humans, cannot synthesize vitamin C.) Some researchers have hypothesized that the skeletal disorders frequently seen in large and giant breeds resemble scurvy, a vitamin C deficiency occurring in humans. However, vitamin C has not been shown to be of any benefit in treating such cases.

Minerals

Minerals, sometimes also called trace elements or micronutrients, are components of bone and teeth and are essential constituents of proteins and fats. They activate the body's enzyme systems and keep the proper level of salts in the bloodstream (*osmotic equilibrium*). The dog requires 22 minerals, seven major ones and 15 *trace* minerals. These trace minerals are tricky, having a narrow safety margin between what is optimal and

what is toxic. Many minerals interrelate with one another, making achieving the correct balance even more difficult. Deficiencies show up rapidly, but the negative effects of excesses can take years to develop and may be irreversible. Minerals can come in various forms. In general, sulfates are more biologically available than carbonates, which are more available than oxides (with the exception of zinc oxide, which is the most common and useful form of supplemented zinc).

Calcium (Ca) and phosphorus (P) are two of the major minerals, and they are closely interrelated. Together they provide over 70 percent of the mineral content of the body, mainly found in bones and teeth. However, calcium is also needed for blood clotting, regulating the heartbeat, and transmitting of

The correct balance of minerals is especially crucial for puppies, with their developing bones.

nerve impulses. Phosphorus plays a role in the transfer and storage of energy in the body and is also a constituent of nucleotides, the precursors of DNA and RNA. The ratio of calcium to phosphorus is crucial, and should be between one-to-one and one and one-half-to-one.

Symptoms of Deficiencies and Excesses of Minerals

Mineral	Deficiency	Excess
Calcium (Ca) and Phosphorus (P)	Skeletal deformities Lameness Eclampsia in lactating bitches	Hip dysplasia Wobbler syndrome Osteochondrosis dessicans
Potassium (K)	Muscular weakness Poor growth (Unlikely to occur)	
Magnesium (Mg)	Muscular weakness Convulsions (Unlikely to occur)	
Sodium (Na), Chlorine (Cl) and Sulfur (S)	Fatigue Exhaustion Decreased water intake Retarded growth	Greater than normal fluid intake
Iron (Fe)	Anemia Weakness Fatigue	Anemia Weight loss
Copper (Cu)	Anemia Bone disorders	In dogs with copper toxicosis, hepatitis and cirrhosis
Manganese (Mn)	Defective growth Reproductive failure Disturbances in fat metabolism	
Zinc (Zn)	Poor growth Anorexia Emaciation Testicular atrophy Poor skin and coat condition	
Iodine (I)	Enlargement of thyroid Apathy Reproductive failure	Same symptoms as deficiency but acute
Selenium (Se)	Degeneration of skeletal and cardiac muscles	Death

The amount of calcium available to the body can be influenced by many things. Some fat is necessary for absorption of calcium, but too much retards absorption. Phytic acid in the bran portion of cereals can combine with calcium as well as other minerals to form insoluble salts. Insoluble salts (for example, calcium oxalate) and excesses of iron, manganese, and zinc result in less efficient absorption of calcium. Vitamin D deficiencies interfere with calcium absorption in the intestine. Vitamin D excesses can result in hypercalcemia, with excesses deposited in bone, then soft tissues, then even heart muscle as the body tries to deal with the overload. Excesses of calcium or phosphorus in growing dogs can result in disastrous skeletal abnormalities (discussed further in Chapter Nine). Do not supplement with calcium or phosphorus unless under instructions of your veterinarian.

Potassium (K) is present in all plant materials. It is essential in protecting the body from infection, and it plays a crucial role (with magnesium, sodium, and chlorine) in the body's fluid balance. The requirement for potassium is linked to the level of protein in the diet, which itself is impacted by many things, as stated above. (You begin to see how intertwined all the separate details of nutrition are.) High-protein diets must include adequate levels of potassium.

Magnesium (Mg), sodium (Na), chlorine (Cl), and sulfur (S) can all be discussed together because their common major role is fluid regulation. You've heard of electrolytes? Well, magnesium and sodium, plus calcium and potassium, are the main cations (positive ions) in the body fluids. Chlorine and sulfur, with bicarbonate and phosphate, comprise the anions (negative ions) of body fluids. Instinctively, you know that these positives and negatives must be kept in balance, that is, the electrolyte balance essential to the body's health. Nearly all the physical and chemical processes of the body depend to some extent on electrolyte balance. Any alteration in the volume of body fluids has an impact on electrolyte concentration. Diarrhea causes substantial losses of sodium, chlorine, and bicarbonate. Vomiting causes loss mainly of chlorine. Any form of prolonged dehydration results in potassium leaching out of the cellular fluid. That is why not just water but electrolytes must be replaced.

Common salt (sodium and chlorine) is the normal source of these two minerals. Magnesium is obtained from legumes, grains, and bonemeal and must be in correct proportions with calcium to ensure normal cardiac, muscular, and nervous functions. Sulfates are the most biologically available forms of inorganic substances, and sulfur is a constituent of amino acids.

With the trace minerals, amounts become even more critical. Some, such as selenium, are toxic at

AAFCO Dog Food Nutrient Profiles
(Presumes an Energy Density of 3.5 kcal ME/g)

Nutrient	Units	Maintenance Minimum	Growth/Reproduction Minimum	Maximum
Proteins	%	18.0	22.0	
Arginine	%	0.51	0.62	
Histidine	%	0.18	0.22	
Isoleucine	%	0.37	0.45	
Leucine	%	0.59	0.72	
Lysine	%	0.63	0.77	
Methionine-Cystine	%	0.43	0.53	
Phenylalanine-tyrosine	%	0.73	0.89	
Threonine	%	0.48	0.58	
Tryptophan	%	0.16	0.20	
Valine	%	0.39	0.48	
Fat	%	5.0	8.0	
Linoleic acid	%	1.0	1.0	
Minerals				
Calcium	%	0.6	1.0	2.5
Phosphorus	%	0.5	0.8	1.6
(Ca:P ratio)		1:1	1:1	2:1
Potassium	%	0.6	0.6	
Sodium	%	0.06	0.3	
Chlorine	%	0.09	0.45	
Magnesium	%	0.04	0.04	0.3

extremely low levels yet are still required by the body. Nearly all interact with each other and with other nutrients, making providing them all in correct concentrations extremely tricky.

Iron (Fe) makes up about two-thirds of the blood's hemoglobin, needed for oxygen transport to the tissues. It is also an essential part of the enzymes involved in nutrient metabolism. Excesses of zinc inter-fere with utilization of iron. Studies done on humans have shown that soy in the diet may also reduce the absorption of iron, as well as manganese and zinc, but canine studies have not yet been performed.

Copper (Cu) is closely linked with the metabolism of iron. Too much copper in the diet can produce iron-deficient anemia by using all the available absorption sites in the intestines. However, copper is itself

AAFCO Dog Food Nutrient Profiles (continued)

Nutrient	Units	Maintenance Minimum	Growth/Reproduction Minimum	Maximum
Iron	mg/kg	80	80	3,000
Copper	mg/kg	7.3	7.3	250
Manganese	mg/kg	5.0	5.0	
Zinc	mg/kg	120	120	1,000
Iodine	mg/kg	1.5	1.5	50
Selenium	mg/kg	0.11	0.11	2
Vitamins				
A	IU/kg	5,000	5,000	250,000
D	IU/kg	500	500	5,000
E	IU/kg	50	50	1,000
Thiamine	mg/kg	1.0	1.0	
Riboflavin	mg/kg	2.2	2.2	
Pantothenic acid	mg/kg	10	10	
Niacin	mg/kg	11.4	11.4	
Pyridoxine	mg/kg	1.0	1.0	
Folic acid	mg/kg	0.18	0.18	
B12	mg/kg	0.022	0.022	
Choline	mg/kg	1,200	1,200	

From AAFCO Official Publication 1997. Used with permission.
(mg/kg = milligrams per kilogram of body weight. IU/kg = International units per kilogram of body weight; International units is a common measure of vitamin dosage. The scientific community generally uses metric measurements, such as kilograms. 1 kilogram = approximately 2.2 pounds.)

essential to blood-forming cells and in the formation of the pigment melanin. Bedlington Terriers and, to a lesser degree, West Highland White Terriers and Doberman Pinschers suffer from an inherited disorder that interferes with utilization of copper and can result in toxic excesses accumulating in the liver.

Manganese (Mn) plays a part in many of the body's enzyme systems, especially those dealing with metals. It is involved in oxygenation of tissues and correct bone formation.

Zinc (Zn) is part of the system responsible for protein and carbohydrate metabolism and is important in the action of two sex hormones (follicle stimulating hormone or FSH and luteinizing hormone or LH). In the female, these hormones stimulate estrogen production. In the male, they stimulate spermatogenesis and secretion of testosterone. On

This German Shorthaired Pointer's energy needs will change as he grows to adulthood, but he will always need all the nutrients in correct proportion.

the average, less than 10 percent of zinc in the diet is absorbed because it is particularly affected by many other nutrients. High levels of calcium, the presence of phytic acid from cereal ingredients, and plant-based proteins all interfere with zinc absorption.

Iodine (I) is involved in regulation of the thyroid hormones. Iodine deficiency kicks the thyroid into high gear. It enlarges and becomes swollen, a condition known as goiter.

Selenium (Se) occurs in meats and cereal grains. It is an essential component of the enzyme glutathione peroxidase, a powerful antioxidant. It protects against lead, cadmium, and mercury poisoning and removes damaging peroxides from body tissues.

Cobalt (Co) has already been mentioned as a component of vitamin B12. Molybdenum (Mo) is an antagonist to copper. Fluorine (F) is yet another constituent of bones and teeth.

Water is perhaps not thought of as a nutrient, but in the short term, it is the most essential element for survival of the animal. Every living cell needs water on an ongoing basis. Nearly 70 percent of the weight of an adult is water. However, normal functioning of the body results in continual water loss through urine and feces, via exchange in the lungs, and even to some extent through the skin. Bulk quantities of water cannot be stored in the body, so a constant supply is needed. The general guideline is 1 milliliter of water for every kilocalorie of energy consumed. So a dog eating 1,000 kcal per day needs 1,000 ml, or approximately one quart, of water. Dogs eating canned food will get a significant quantity of water in their food; those eating dry kibble will not. With free access to water, most healthy dogs will keep themselves in fluid balance.

Daily Requirements

Each nutrient must be provided on a plateau between deficiency and toxicity, in the appropriate ratio to the food's energy content and other nutrients, and in a form usable by the dog. One of the most important dietary considerations is that the food satisfy the dog's daily energy needs. The energy density of a food is thus very important. With a balanced commercial diet if the energy needs are met, all the individual nutrient needs should also be met.

Points to Remember

- The recommended daily allowance is only a guideline. A dog's actual requirements will vary depending on life stage, health status, exercise, and environmental conditions.
- The dog's daily energy needs are the basic requirements to fill.
- Metabolizable energy (ME) is the actual energy obtained from the diet by the dog.
- Larger dogs require fewer kilocalories per pound of body weight than do smaller dogs.
- Proteins in the diet must provide the ten essential amino acids.
- A protein's chemical score is based on the essential amino acid in shortest supply. If a particular protein provides only 60 percent of arginine and 100 percent of the nine others, its chemical score is 60.
- Enzymes, a combination of proteins and vitamins, are necessary to break down complex food molecules during digestion.
- Carbohydrates can supply energy and spare protein to be used in cell-building processes.
- Fiber should be moderately fermentable with low solubility to facilitate production of short-chain fatty acids (SCFAs), which play a role in the health of the gastrointestinal tract. Beet pulp and rice bran are good choices.
- Fats are necessary for absorption of fat-soluble vitamins.
- The essential fatty acids linoleic acid and alpha-linolenic acid must be supplied in the diet.
- The fat-soluble vitamins—A, D, E, and K—can be stored in body tissues. Oversupply in the diet can result in toxicities.
- The water-soluble vitamins—thiamine, riboflavin, niacin, pyridoxine, pantothenic acid, biotin, folic acid, choline, B12, and C—are continually washed out of the body. Deficiencies can result if sufficient amounts are not supplied in the diet.
- Antibiotics and feeding of raw egg whites can bind biotin, render it biologically unavailable, and result in deficiencies.
- The dog requires 22 minerals. These minerals have complex interrelationships and narrow ranges of safety. The major ones include calcium, phosphorus, potassium, magnesium, sodium, chlorine, and sulfur. The trace minerals include iron, copper, manganese, zinc, iodine, selenium, cobalt, molybdenum, fluorine, chromium, nickel, silicon, vanadium, and arsenic.
- The calcium-to-phosphorus ratio is crucial and should be between one-to-one and one and one-half-to-one.
- Plentiful clean water should always be supplied. It is the most essential nutrient of all.

Chapter Six

The Canine Connoisseur

Dog food comes in four basic forms, two quite prevalent and two more limited. Dry and canned foods can be found nearly everywhere. Semimoist and frozen foods are more limited in their distribution. The variety of flavors and flavor combinations seems to grow every year. Is all this really necessary for an animal that is known for happily eating garbage and even more repulsive substances? Do canine connoisseurs actually exist?

Many dogs will eat whatever's put in front of them, but some are choosy about their food.

Well, there's no question that dogs have taste. In fact, four groups of taste buds have been identified in the dog. Sugar-sensitive group A receptors are the most abundant. If you find this odd in a so-called carnivore, consider it another indication of the dog's truer status as an omnivore. Wild foxes and coyotes are known to show a definite taste for fruit. To provide the most energy, fruits should be eaten when ripe, meaning high in sugar. Taste buds that react to sugar are essential in making such a determination. The cat—a true carnivore—does not have sugar-sensitive taste buds.

The acid units, group B taste buds, are actually the second most abundant group of taste buds, but their activity level is low. They respond to odd substances such as distilled water and inorganic acids.

Group C taste buds, the nucleotide receptors, respond to the taste of meat. They can be found in dogs, cats, and human beings, among others.

Group D, the furamol receptors, are a second group of taste buds that discern sweetness, in this case specifically fruity sweetness. Interestingly, the dog has no taste buds to receive the flavor of salt. Though sodium is essential, the dog's mostly meat diet provides salt automatically. The dog does not need to identify it and seek it out.

However, this is all physiological information. Does a dog have actual food preferences, likes and dislikes? Most dog owners can tell you their dog's favorite food, so it seems the answer is yes.

Variety in the Canine Diet

In the wild, canines (and felines) are ruled by two powerful drives regarding food. The first drive is against variety—if you've learned how to catch and eat one kind of prey, and it is meeting your needs and all your nutritional requirements are being filled, why risk poisoning or injury by trying new things? Better to be safe and stick with what you know. This has actually been demonstrated in wolf relocation programs. Canadian wolves moved to parks in the United States continued to feed on their customary prey where possible even though new prey species were now available to them.

The second drive is in direct opposition, pro variety. If you learn to feed on only one or two items and one or both of those items becomes scarce or disappears, you will be at a serious disadvantage. Better to sample a lot of possibilities and know what's available.

Chris Thorne, Senior Behaviorist at the Waltham Centre for Pet Nutrition, has investigated the issue of variety in both cats and dogs. "If you feed a cat two different foods and it shows a clear preference for one, then we feed that food for two days and repeat the preference test, the preference is gone. It happens in dogs as well, but where in cats the preference can turn completely around in forty-eight hours, in the dog it takes three weeks. Dogs respond positively to variety in their diet, just not to the same extreme."

Thorne also notes that while, in general, dogs are not as finicky as cats, substantial differences occur between breeds and between individuals. The common conception is that the smaller lap dogs are the fussy ones, twisting their owners around their paws and demanding different taste treats. This is true to some extent. However, Thorne has found that Cavalier King Charles Spaniels are actually gluttonous eaters and Great Danes prove to be quite finicky. Individual canines may also differ from their breed tendencies—believe it or not, some Labs *are* fussy eaters.

So, does your dog need variety? If he or she eats a food with gusto for a month or so then starts leaving it over or even refusing to eat at

What you feed a dog early in life can play a major role in lifelong likes and dislikes.

vegetarian diet, and the third group ate a mixed meat and vegetables diet. The soybean-fed group would not eat any novel foods at all. Those fed the mixed vegetarian diet would sample new vegetables and grains but would not eat any animal protein. The dogs fed the most diversified diet would accept any new food as long as it wasn't bitter or stale in taste. So some early experience with variety is important.

Even with a varied diet history, a bad experience with a food can lead to problems. Cautious dogs may take one bad food experience as reason to reject novelty. Extreme cases may fixate on one food, refusing to eat even that if the manufacturer changes the formulation.

In a direct contradiction to the dog trainer's insistence that reward or punishment must be closely connected to the deed, dogs seem quite capable of connecting an eating experience with an unpleasant physiological effect that occurs hours or even days afterward. A toxic substance may sicken a dog quickly, but a nutritionally inadequate diet may take a week or even longer to show ill effects. Yet the dog can make the association between the ultimate outcome and the food and will demonstrate an aversion to the food if offered it again.

Dogs do have some general likes and dislikes. A sweet taste, often associated with a high level of carbohydrates, is preferred. The bitter taste present in many toxic materials is avoided. Dogs prefer meat over

all (and no health problems are present), your dog may be asking for a change of menu.

With a dog that craves monotony, you may see an opposite response. The dog is eating the same old food happily every day, but the owner decides that must be boring and serves a new food. The dog may nibble tentatively or refuse to try it at all. This is not necessarily a reflection on the food. Cautious dogs regard novel food items as risky, perhaps nutritionally inadequate or even toxic. Some may eat a small amount to try to assess the food's suitability. After a few days of this, the dog may begin to eat the food, having added it to the list of acceptable foods. Others may refuse even to try the new food.

Dietary history can figure into the dog's response to novel foods. One study used three groups of Chow Chow puppies. From weaning to six months, one group was fed a soybean diet, one was given a mixed

vegetable protein. Taste preference studies at dog food manufacturers' research facilities have ranked meats, with beef the preferred meat, followed by pork, lamb, chicken, and horse meat. Unexpectedly, they also found that dogs preferred cooked meat to raw and canned meat over freshly cooked.

Specific food preferences appear to result from both individual experience and a genetic predisposition. Researchers have been able to increase or decrease food preferences through inbreeding. This also agrees with the differences seen between breeds. While breeding to select for ear set, coat color and length, size, and so on, we have also bred in tendencies toward fussiness or gluttony.

Some dog food manufacturers still maintain that changing a dog's or cat's diet will create a finicky eater. You could change foods too often, of course, but having a dog that accepts new foods, or even campaigns for them occasionally, is preferable to a dog stuck on only one kind of food. What happens if the company discontinues the product or goes out of business?

Veterinarians critical of the pet food industry insist that pet foods are not as "complete and balanced" as the manufacturers would have us believe. They advise that changing foods every couple of months is a good plan to avoid nutritional deficiencies. Always remember to change foods gradually to avoid risks of digestive upset.

Offering a food by hand makes it much more exciting and valuable to a dog.

When changing your dog's basic diet, mix a little of the new food with a much larger quantity of the old food. Gradually increase the percentage of new food until, after two or three weeks, you have completely switched to the new food. The bacterial flora in your dog's digestive tract need time to adjust to new formulations and ingredients.

If you feed a mix of foods, such as a bowl of dry with some canned mixed in, you should be able to change flavors of canned food day to day with no problems, especially if you stay with the same brand. This is one of the reasons pet food companies offer such a variety of flavors.

Jim Sokolowski, DVM, Ph.D., professional services manager at

Characteristics of Different Types of Dog Foods

	Dry	Canned	Semimoist	Frozen
Percent of moisture	7–10	70–80	15–30	40–50
Feed free choice?	Yes	No	No	No
Level of preservatives	High	Low	Some, plus humectants	Low
Refrigerate?	No	Once opened	No	Yes
Variety within a product line	Some	Yes	No	Some
Palatability	High to low	High	High	High when warmed
Cost	Varies much, but generally lower than other forms	Generally moderate	Between dry and canned	High

Waltham USA, points out that our cultural influences also affect our dogs. "Our palate prejudices as owners figure into what we *think* our dogs want to eat, and ultimately we choose which food goes into their bowls." Thus, dogs in Mexico are more likely to accept spicy foods, even chilies. French canines may routinely eat horse meat, though in the U.S. market, many pet owners balk at the idea of feeding horses to dogs. In the Arctic, dogs often dine on fish and seal meat.

One last item of note—dogs are more likely to eat any item of food if it is fed to them by hand. The interaction with the owner greatly increases the value of the food, a useful note to remember if you have to give your dog pills and want to hide them in some meat or cheese rather than forcing them down the dog's throat.

Dry, Canned, Semimoist, or Frozen?

By far, the majority of dog food sold in the United States is dry, accounting for 80 to 90 percent of sales. Is this simply a matter of convenience or economics? Let's do a basic comparison first.

Odor, taste, and texture all play important roles in the dog's acceptance of a food. Though canned food has an intrinsic advantage, each form has foods with good palatability. Because dry is by far the most popular form, we will discuss it first.

Dry Dog Food

Dry food is easy to store, even when purchased in bulk. Bag sizes range from four to 40 pounds, and packaging adds little to the cost. With its low moisture content, dry food is energy dense. A smaller quantity meets the dog's energy requirements. It may be fed free choice but is more often offered as a meal once or twice a day.

Some dogs do prefer food in dry form. Something called *mouth feel* factors into a food's attractiveness, and some canines prefer the crunch of kibble. This same quality may also assist in cleaning tartar from teeth and maintaining healthy gums, but only in dogs that actually chew their kibble.

Stool quantity and quality are generally good with dry foods. The lower quantity fed can mean fewer feces, but this depends to a large extent on the food's digestibility, which can vary greatly from one food to another. If the piles of poop in your yard might lead people to believe you're harboring an elephant rather than an elkhound, the food's digestibility is probably low. You may want to consider switching brands. Though the price of your current brand may seem a bargain, you are paying for a lot of ingredients your dog's digestive tract can't use. A food with higher digestibility will mean you feed less, so though the price per pound may be higher, the same size bag will last longer. Your dog will also produce less excrement, surely a welcome additional benefit.

Dry food comes in several forms. Meals or flakes are rare but still

seen. Before the 1960s, they comprised the bulk of the dry foods available. A few manufacturers still maintain that meals or flakes are more healthful than the now common extruded foods. Dried, flaked, and granular ingredients are prepared separately and blended to make the final product.

When meals were the major dry dog food, they did not exactly provide superb canine nutrition. Ground corn, cracked wheat, and rolled oats were mixed with some dried *tankage*, and a mix of vitamins and minerals were added. (Tankage refers, according to AAFCO, to residues from animal tissues, including bones and exclusive of hair, hoofs, horns, and the contents

If you decide you're going to feed dry, you can choose among dozens of brands and flavors.

Canned food can keep a dog in prime condition.

of the digestive tract.) Today, the blend may contain cornmeal, wheat flakes, and oatmeal, all cooked to render them more digestible, and meat and bone meal with a reliable protein and fat content. Or it may be more exotic millet, rice, and flaxseed mixed with lamb meat and menhaden fish meal.

Are meals or flakes somehow more healthful than extruded foods, as their manufacturers claim? David Dzanis of the FDA's Center for Veterinary Medicine states, "Some people say that because meals are baked not extruded they preserve the nutritional content better. But how a food is formulated has more impact than how it's cooked. Meals are denser because extruded has air in it. Think of Grape Nuts versus Captain Crunch cereal."

Biscuits and kibbles still exist, though they are also rare. Both of these products are made in the same fashion as bread or cookies—

all the ingredients are blended into a dough and then baked. Biscuits are cut into individual shapes before baking. For kibble, the dough is baked in flat sheets, then broken into bite-sized pieces of roughly the same size. Some kibbles are bounced over screens after being broken to allow smaller particles, called *fines*, to drop away before the kibbles are packaged.

However, by far the most widely used process for manufacturing dry foods is extrusion. As with biscuits and kibbles, the ingredients are mixed to form a dough, but here the mixing is done inside a pressure cooker. The ingredients are steam cooked while they are blended. The dough is pushed through a die to form shapes. A coating of fat is sprayed onto the shapes, and they are dried to nugget hardness. Because of the fat coating, these foods must be packaged in bags where the innermost wall serves as a grease barrier. The extrusion process itself requires that the formulation be high in carbohydrates; binders such as cellulose gums or lignin extracts are sometimes added to further improve consistency. The combination of heat, steam, and pressure cooks the starches well—maximizing their digestibility and palatability.

The manufacturer's care during production is essential. Harsh or improper cooking and drying can result in loss of nutrients, lower palatability, or even lower digestibility.

Fermentability and Solubility of Fiber Sources

Fiber	Solubility	Fermentability
Beet pulp	Low	Moderate
Cellulose	Low	Low
Rice bran	Low	Moderate
Gum arabic	High	Moderate
Pectin	Low	High
C-M cellulose	High	Low
Methylcellulose	High	Low
Cabbage fiber	Low	High
Guar gum	High	High
Locust bean gum	High	Low
Xanthan gum	High	Moderate

From Iams. June 1994. Advances in Fiber Nutrition. *Topics in Practical Nutrition.* Vol. 4, No. 2. Used with permission.

Canned Dog Food

Canned food is easy to store while sealed but must be refrigerated once opened. It is highly palatable, generally higher in fats than dry foods, and has a high moisture content. The dog may need to eat a larger quantity to receive the needed quantity of nutrients. Canned food cannot be fed free choice, because it will spoil if left out.

Most dogs devour canned food eagerly. Owners enjoy seeing their dogs enjoy the food, but should be prepared to perform frequent toothbrushing. Canned food tends to stick to teeth and gums and can hasten dental problems if not cleaned away. It also leads to more pungent doggy breath.

Stool quality can vary widely. Many canned foods contain little or no carbohydrate or fiber, and these formulations can result in softer stools. Dogs unused to eating canned food often suffer diarrhea if suddenly provided with a canned food diet.

Canned food may come in the form of a loaf, chunks in gravy, or stew. Loaf products include more carbohydrates and fibers than the other forms. The ingredients are ground and blended together with fats and water. The higher percentage of carbohydrates binds the mixture into a solid loaf.

Chunks in gravy products have their ingredients chopped rather than ground, and the mixture is extruded into chunks. Gum arabic, xanthan gum, and vegetable gums may be added to help the chunks congeal. Color enhancers such as caramel may be added to improve the appearance of the product.

For stews, whole peas and carrot chunks are added to chunks in gravy. These products are highly appealing to dog owners, some looking good enough to serve for their own dinner.

All forms of canned food are cooked in a two-stage process. While ingredients are blended, they are steam cooked. Once the contents are poured into the can, they are pressure cooked, typically held at 250 degrees for an hour. Minimal nutrient loss occurs—mainly thiamine, which is extremely heat sensitive.

Though feeding a diet solely of canned food is three times as expensive as feeding dry food, there is a tendency to overfeed. While dogs are enthusiastic about freshly opened cans, they are less than thrilled with cold, dried-out leftovers. Owners most often ladle out all the contents of the can, whether or not this is an appropriate amount for the dog. An increased variety of can sizes has helped somewhat.

The high moisture content of canned foods releases both flavor and odor, encouraging dogs to eat. For anorectic dogs or those with tooth or mouth problems, canned food may prove helpful.

Semimoist Dog Food

Moisture content in semimoist dog food ranges from 15 to 30 percent. To prevent spoilage, humectants are added. These substances—simple sugars, corn syrup, or glycerol—bind the water molecules in the food, protecting the food from bacterial and fungal activity. Preservatives are also added to prevent mold or yeast growth. All of this protection means that semimoist foods are not a good choice for consumers concerned about artificial substances in their dog foods. (Interestingly, propylene glycol was determined to be a risk to cats and has been prohibited in cat foods but can still be used in dog foods.)

Semimoist foods are shaped and colored in a variety of ways meant to resemble different cuts or types of meat. Some are formed into hamburger-like patties, while others are packaged in *ground* form not shaped into patties. There are chunks meant to invoke images of cut-up steak, and even more elaborate *ribbon* chunks. These have a white stripe of "fat" running across each chunk.

Individual packages generally contain relatively small quantities of food, so feeding the correct amount is easily accomplished. Though the product seems fairly odorless to humans, it appears to have an attractive, meaty smell to dogs. The product dries and becomes unappetizing if left out, so it is not a good option for free choice feeding.

Refrigerated/Frozen Dog Food

Most seldom seen is the refrigerated/frozen type of dog food. Some products are meant to be fed as the complete diet and others more as training lures/rewards. However, they comprise a very small piece of the dog food market.

Proponents of frozen food like to point out that this form does not have to be processed at high temperatures, thus sparing nutrients from destruction. While this is true, manufacturers of dry, semimoist, and canned foods take the effects of heat into account in their formulations.

One immense drawback is that these foods must be kept in the refrigerator or the freezer. Those that are frozen must be defrosted before they will be needed. Both should preferably be heated to room temperature before being fed. This takes planning.

If these foods are heated before serving, they are quite palatable and may encourage overeating. They would be quite expensive to feed as the only form of food. Some of the owners who breed and show their dogs insist that these foods are more natural and improve their dogs' coats and condition.

Mixing

A survey of dog owners found that while the vast majority reported feeding dry dog food, 90 percent of those also said they added something to the dry food. Some foods suggest that owners add warm water to make a gravy, and some owners reported that they did just that. Others, however, added gravy or stock of their own, canned food, or even table scraps. People seemed to want to be more involved in the process of

Here, a dog owner adds homemade chicken broth to dry food.

feeding their dogs than simply transferring some dry food from a bag to a bowl. Of course, the dogs play their part by showing more enjoyment when added enticements are mixed into their kibble.

One study even found that dry and canned foods fed together were digested more efficiently than either one alone. Conjecture is that the dog's digestive tract produces an improved blend of enzymes in response to this food combination, but no one knows for sure.

If you are going to mix canned and dry, follow these guidelines:
• To start adding canned food for the first time, progress slowly. The sudden addition of canned food in too large a quantity can cause diarrhea.
• Try to use dry and canned products from the same manufacturer. This way, the nutritional formulations will be coordinated. If you don't want to follow this advice, then choose products with similar fat and protein profiles.

- If you are feeding a special dry food, such as lite or senior, adding other foods can cancel the low-calorie or special-formula benefits of the dry diet. You can often find canned products to meet these special needs and can mix them with the dry food without qualms.

Canine nutritionists recommend using a mix of 75 percent dry and 25 percent canned, by volume. This is remarkably close to the actual percentages of dry and canned food sold.

Canned foods are offered in a wide panoply of flavors by each pet food manufacturer, so adding canned is a simple way to provide variety in your dog's diet. In general, a change in flavor is unlikely to cause digestive upsets, though occasionally a novel ingredient may result in some temporarily loose stools.

Consider one caveat when searching for variety for your dog's dinner—if food allergies occur and you have fed your dog every food formulation on the market, devising a diet that contains novel ingredients to soothe the allergies will be difficult. Don't feed a rabbit and potatoes diet just because one exists. Leave something in reserve.

Even some owners who don't add canned to dry advocate some sort of moistening. They think that not only does moistening increase palatability, it expands the dry food before the dog eats it. Some people insist that this is an important step in the prevention of bloat, while oth-ers say that it helps decrease consumption of food by providing more bulk. Thus far, no evidence confirms or refutes the bloat hypothesis. David Dzanis of the FDA's Center for Veterinary Medicine notes, "Wetting a dry food means that you can't leave it out, you have to get rid of it faster. But it does improve the mouth feel of the product." So it is possible that a dog may be happier having his dry food wetted.

Table Scraps, or "People" Food

In years gone by, a pet's entire diet often consisted of table scraps. Of course, years ago our own diets were less processed and less packaged, and table scraps actually had nutritional value. Nowadays, table scraps are likely to contain calories and little else in the way of nutrients. So, are table scraps a forbidden food? No, but use common sense and moderation.

Plenty of people prefer to put the trimmings from their steak onto the pet's plate rather than into the trash. This should do no harm if done sensibly. Iams recommends that table scraps provide no more than 5 to 10 percent of the dog's daily caloric intake. But you're unlikely to know how many calories are in that chunk of baked potato with sour cream and that morsel of pork chop. A more realistic instruction is simply to include table scraps occasionally, not on a regular basis, and in small amounts.

Do not use table scraps in an effort to encourage a finicky pooch to eat. Unless you go to the extreme of grinding the commercially prepared food and the scraps together in a blender or food processor, the dog will likely eat the table scraps and leave the prepared food behind. This is not a balanced diet.

There are also some table scraps you simply should not give a dog. You've undoubtedly heard that bones are a bad idea (plenty of good alternatives will be discussed in the Treats section next). They can lodge anywhere from the mouth to the intestines, or splinter and puncture vital organs. If for some reason you feel you must give the dog a bone, at least buy the sterilized bones available at pet stores or ask your butcher for a knuckle bone. These choices are less inclined to splinter.

Chocolate is also a forbidden food. The theobromine in chocolate can cause serious health effects, ranging from vomiting to irregular heartbeat and death. The darker the chocolate, the more theobromine it contains, so bittersweet and baking chocolate are particularly hazardous. Dogs can safely consume the chocolate substitute carob.

Other foods can cause less-well-known problems. Eating onions can actually result in destruction of red blood cells in dogs, which can cause anemia (though the quantity would have to be large). Any people

Feeding a dog from the table can encourage begging. If you're going to give scraps, either add them to the dog's dinner or offer by hand away from the table.

foods can upset the nutritional balance of a manufactured food, may lead to obesity, and could encourage begging for or even stealing food. When feeding people food, moderation is the watchword if you just can't manage abstinence.

Treats

Treats is yet another burgeoning area in the world of pet foods. In the 1990s, dog owners are spending more than half a billion dollars a year on treats. More than half of dog owners readily admit to giving treats. However, a hard core third or slightly more account for a whopping 75 percent of treat purchases.

These people in particular, and dog owners in general, should know that too many treats can cause nutritional problems. Many contain high proportions of fat and sugar, just as our desserts. Treats

should be held to less than 5 percent of daily caloric intake. But there is nothing wrong with treats in moderation.

The variety of treats available is overwhelming. In the supermarket and feed store, you can find shelves full of biscuits, chews, and all sorts of treats. Many are sold by the same manufacturers as those selling canned and dry food on the next shelf lower down. A quick scan reveals biscuits as simple as Milkbones or as fancy as Bonz, tiny People Crackers, or heavenly vanilla Hartz Scrumptious Dog Kookies. Chews might include strips of rawhide, logs of compressed rawhide, pigs' ears, cows' hooves, or bone-shaped products made of various vegetables. Then there are all types and sizes of jerky offerings, Pedigree's special tooth-cleaning DentaBones, vitamin drops, and who knows what else.

But these sources barely scratch the surface. Venture into the large pet supply superstores, catalog sales, or the new doggie bakeries springing up around the country and your mind will truly boggle. The menu at places such as Three Dog Bakery or Dinger's Dog Bakery might feature Big Scary Kitties, Beagle Bagels, Carob Hearts, Veggie Bonz, Mini Pupcakes, and more. Personalized birthday cakes and gift baskets are available and many products are offered through mail order catalogs.

You can buy a liquid bottled like Worcestershire to be poured over food for flavor enhancement. There are mixes for baking your own biscuits. There are vegetarian biscuits. There are even treats specially formulated to be for dogs on special diets because of kidney or heart problems, diabetes, allergies, or gastrointestinal disorders.

Trends being seen in the area of treats are moves toward more natural products and fast increasing sales of soft, meaty treats. The popularity of pigs' ears has led to other such doggie delicacies, including Choo-hooves (sterilized cows' hooves), pig snouts, Lammy Whammies, and others. Biscuits remain popular, as do jerky treats. Hard chews are useful both for occupying a dog's time and for helping to scrape away plaque and tartar. Knuckle bones from the butcher and sterilized bone segments sold in packages are two of the oldest choices. They were followed by rawhide, another natural product. For some dogs, rawhide is a fine choice, but others try to swallow a chunk without enough chewing and could choke. Some dogs have digestive upsets, and chemicals used on the cowhides from which the rawhide comes have caused problems. Rawhide also becomes very sticky when chewed and may stain carpet. It also can be covered in dirt and hair if nosed around a less-than-immaculate floor.

Nylabones, a synthetic bone that a dog can chew and swallow but not digest, was an early innovation. Nylabones have the advantage of lasting a long time and not adding any calories to the dog's diet. However, people have complained about some splintering as the product ages. Some dog owners object to "feeding" an oil derivative (Nylabones are plastic) to their dogs.

Choo-hooves are another castoff from animals raised for human consumption, this one being sterilized cow hooves. Some dogs find them quite enticing, but others pay no attention to them. Choo-hooves last a long time but can have problems with splintering.

Booda Velvets are promoted, without actually naming names, as an advancement on Nylabones. They are made from cornstarch and so are biodegradable, though not digestible. Though they are attractive and dogs seem to like them, Booda Velvets can splinter. Broken-off pieces are even more magnetic to dirt and hair than is rawhide.

Compressed rawhide—rawhide that is ground up then pressed together—avoids the problems with potential choking and does not become sticky when chewed. Dogs mostly love it, and it has some good teeth-cleaning properties. Compressed rawhide is a good choice, though it does not last as long as the harder chews.

The latest innovations as of this writing are Pedigree Dentabones and Nylabone Carrot-Bones. Dentabones have been available in England for years (as Rask) but only recently came to the United States. Made mainly of rice, they are an

Dogs can enjoy rawhide but should be supervised.

oddly shaped, quite hard chew that is digestible. Their abrasive texture effectively cleans teeth, and they do not splinter when chewed. Offer the large size so that it is gnawed rather than broken into pieces for best results.

Nylabone Carrot-Bones claims to be the world's first vegetable bone. It is a crunchy bone composed of carrots and other natural ingredients, with no plastics or artificial anything. It is a good choice for dogs fighting obesity, as it is lower in calories than many other treats. It is also good for dogs with medical conditions requiring lower protein.

No matter what hard treat you and your dog may choose, it is best to supervise the dog's chewing activity. Teeth can be occasionally broken by these products, some products can splinter, and some may cause choking.

Some fairly new products are meant to dispense treats to a dog left alone at home. Dog trainers started this idea by advising their clients to take a dog toy called Kong and stuff its central hole with kibble and peanut butter. Trying to extract the treats would keep a dog occupied and help to avoid destructive behaviors while the owners were away.

That idea developed into cubes, balls, and disks specifically designed to hold treats and make a dog work to get at them. These devices can be a boon to dog owners who must leave dogs at home while they go off to work.

Treats are regulated by all the same agencies as dog food, but the guidelines are much less strict. As long as the main display panel clearly identifies the product as a snack or treat and packaging proclaims that "This product is intended for intermittent or supplemental feeding only," treats do not have to meet any sort of nutritional adequacy guidelines.

One reason for the rising popularity of treats is the rising popularity of food training. By its very name, food training indicates using a lot of food in the training process. Some people simply use their dog's regular dry food, deducting the amount from the daily ration. This is the simplest way to be sure you aren't supplying excess nutrition or an unbalanced diet. However, some dogs are not motivated by the same old kibble.

An alternate plan is to find a loaf-style canned food similar in nutritional value to your dry food, or if you feed canned, choose a loaf-style. Remove the product from the can, slice it thin, and bake it in a slow oven until it is completely dry. Crumble and use as treats, remembering to deduct comparable calories from your dog's meal. You can use the same technique with frozen/refrigerated roll type foods.

If you do use treats of some sort, choose those without a lot of preservatives, humectants, and stabilizers. Remember that treats contain calories.

Points to Remember

- Dogs have taste buds responding to sugars and may enjoy grapes, watermelon, cantaloupe, and other fruits as treats.
- Canines are ruled by conflicting drives regarding variety in their diet. New foods are an unknown, are potentially hazardous, and should be avoided. However, variety is important in case one type of food supply disappears. Some dogs will refuse even to try new things, while some will reject a food after a month in search of variety.
- Dry food is economical, easy to store, and may be fed free choice (to dogs who do not overeat).
- Canned food is highly palatable, has fewer preservatives, and comes in a wide variety of styles and flavors.
- Semimoist food is neat and easy to feed, with good palatability, but is high in artificial substances.
- Refrigerated/frozen food is rare but an energy dense, highly palatable food that must, obviously, be kept under refrigeration.
- Mixing types of food is fine. In fact, this may increase both owner and canine enjoyment of the meal.
- Table scraps, if given, should be an occasional treat offered in small quantities only.
- Hazardous substances such as small bones, which can splinter, and chocolate, which is toxic to dogs, should never be given.
- Treats contain calories and must be accounted for in the dog's daily food intake. Food trainers, in particular, using many treats daily, must be careful not to overfeed their dogs.

Chapter Seven

Ingredients and Other Issues

Trying to assess the ingredients in a dog food may seem like an impossible task. The words are unfamiliar and even when you do understand them, they don't provide much information about quality. The confusion doesn't involve just ingredients, either. Just what is a *premium* food? Are preservatives a necessary evil, just necessary, or just evil?

This is a large subject but also one that can certainly help in your evaluation of dog food. We will tackle it by first looking at typical ingredients lists from different price categories of dry foods and then providing tables of nutrient profiles for a variety of ingredients. We will examine the issues of supplementing your dog's food, possible contaminants, how to store food safely, and the preservatives and antioxidants that have been debated for years. The chapter wraps up with a discussion of topics on the fringe, such as mad cow disease and pets as pet food ingredients.

Some Typical Ingredients Lists

Ross Becker, the editor of *Good Dog!* magazine, which frequently reviews and discusses dog food, devised the categories of economy, premium, super-premium II, and super-premium I. They will be explained in the glossary. These are partial lists only, providing the major ingredients of each food.

Economy Food

Ground yellow corn, soy flour, soybean meal, meat and bone meal, wheat flour, corn syrup, animal fat. Guaranteed analysis: crude protein (min.) 19%, crude fat (min.) 8%, crude fiber (max.) 4%, moisture (max.) 18% 326 kcal/cup.

Premium Food

Ground yellow corn, chicken by-product meal, feeding oatmeal, soybean meal, animal fat, digest of poultry by-products and beef and beef by-products, brewers rice.

Guaranteed analysis: crude protein (min.) 22%, crude fat (min.) 8%, crude fiber (max.) 4%, moisture (max.) 10%. 338 kcal/cup.

Super-Premium II Foods

Poultry by-products, ground yellow corn, poultry by-product meal, wheat flour, oat flour, chicken, poultry fat preserved with mixed tocopherols and citric acid, beet pulp, whole egg, brewers rice, wheat germ meal, flaxseed. Guaranteed analysis: crude protein (min.) 22%, crude fat (min.) 15%, crude fiber (max.) 4%, moisture (max.) 10%. 386 kcal/cup.

Super-Premium I Foods

Turkey, chicken, chicken meal, whole ground barley, whole ground brown rice, whole steamed potatoes, ground white rice, chicken fat preserved with natural vitamin E and vitamin C, herring meal, whole raw apple, whole steamed carrots, cottage cheese, sunflower oil, dicalcium phosphate, alfalfa sprouts, whole eggs with shells, whole clove garlic, vitamin C. Guaranteed analysis: crude protein (min.) 24%, crude fat (min.) 14%, crude fiber (max.) 3%, moisture (max.) 10%. 558 kcal/cup.

By perusing the ingredients and guaranteed analysis between groups, you can get a basic idea of how you feel about what should go into your dog's food. If you're going to go by either pure appeal of ingredients or how high the meat ingredients come in the ingredients list, you're going to choose the super-

premium I food. Before you respond that such a food will be too high priced for your wallet, consider the whopping caloric density of 558 kcal per cup, far higher than any of the other foods presented here. This indicates a nutrient-dense product, highly digestible. You will, in fact, have to be careful about the amount fed to avoid canine weight gain. You will feed more meals out of one bag of super-premium I dog food than you would with the other foods.

This comparison of kilocalories of metabolizable energy per cup is actually a fast and reasonably accurate way of assessing the bioavailability and digestibility of a food's ingredients. Unfortunately, not all foods provide the kilocalories per cup figure on their packaging (they have only been permitted to do so since January 1997). You can either choose a food that does include this

Feeding a dog involves a lot more than just fitting the dog to the bowl.

information or call the manufacturer's toll-free number and ask.

Note that no reference to *quality* of ingredients is permitted in the ingredients list on labels. The information panel may include statements about the *benefits* of ingredients. Any health-related claims can be reviewed by the FDA.

To make matters even more confusing, meat even from a single animal can vary widely in its qualities depending on the site from which the meat is taken. The amino acid profile, digestibility, fat content, and degree of saturation can all differ from one cut of meat to another. Reputable manufacturers constantly check their ingredients to ensure correct levels of nutrients.

Manufacturers' literature may include information about digestibility, information not permitted on the product label. A dry matter digestibility of 75 to 80 percent is good.

Nutrient Profiles

Next, a couple of tables present the nutrient profiles of some ingredients commonly found in dog food.

Nutrient Profiles of Selected Ingredients

Ingredient	% crude Protein	% Crude Fat	% Crude Fiber	% Crude Carbohydrate
Poultry by-product meal	58.4	12.4	2.3	5.3
Chicken (whole carcass)	19.9	12.1	n/a	n/a
Meat meal	53.8	9.0	2.4	3.0
Fish meal	64.8	6.0	0.8	n/a
Beef with bone meal	50.5	9.9	2.0	2.2
Eggs (without shells)	12.8	11.4	n/a	0.9
Corn (avg. whole grain)	9.6	3.9	2.1	71.1
Corn gluten meal	43.1	2.2	4.5	38.0
Wheat (avg. whole grain)	14.9	1.8	2.5	67.3
Wheat gluten meal	49.8	4.4	6.0	25.2
Soybean hulls	11.0	2.2	37.3	37.0
Soybean meal	40.1	0.9	6.3	37.3
Rice (ground)	8.4	1.7	9.1	65.1
Rice hulls	2.8	0.7	40.1	29.8
Oats (avg. whole grain)	12.1	4.9	10.9	58.0
Oatmeal	14.7	6.5	4.4	63.1
Oat hulls	3.6	1.6	31.0	50.6
Beet pulp	8.7	0.5	17.9	58.1
Peanut hulls	6.1	1.0	53.9	26.7

Typical Nutrient Content of Some Meats and Meat By-products

Raw Lean Meat	% Crude Protein	% Crude Fat	% Water
Pork	20.6	7.1	71.5
Beef	20.3	4.6	74.0
Lamb	20.8	8.8	70.1
Veal	21.1	2.7	74.9
Chicken	20.6	4.3	74.4
Duck	19.7	4.8	75.0
Turkey	21.9	2.2	75.5
Rabbit	21.9	4.0	74.6
Offal			
Udders	11.0	15.3	72.4
Lungs*	17.2	5.0	73.1
Brains	10.3	7.6	79.4
Kidney*	15.7	2.6	79.8
Heart	14.3	15.5	70.1
Liver*	21.1	7.8	68.6
Tripe*	9.0	3.0	88.0

(*Lungs are designated as *fatty* lungs; kidney is beef; liver is fresh; and tripe is dressed.)
Table adapted from Waltham Centre for Pet Nutrition, *The Waltham Book of Companion Animal Nutrition*. Used with permission.

One means of assessing protein quality is by hydroxyproline content. Never mind what it is—just understand that the higher the hydroxyproline, the lower the protein quality.

Hydroxyproline Content of Some Protein Sources

Protein Source	Hydroxyproline (%)
Egg	0.0
Poultry byproduct meal	3.2
Chicken meal	4.5
Meat meal	5.8
Lamb meal	6.2
Collagen	13.9

Supplements, Contaminants, and Malnutrition

In the United States, where dogs are generally maintained on high-quality, commercial dog foods, cases of malnutrition are rare. In countries where dogs must exist on table scraps, poor-quality commercial diets, or even garbage, of course many more problems occur. For U.S. dogs, the main causes of malnutrition are

- Outdated, badly stored, or contaminated food
- Generic dog food
- Table scraps
- Insufficient food or excessive competition for it

Properly storing dog food is crucial to avoid rancidity, insect infestation, and other problems.

- Excessive supplementation of specific nutrient(s)
- Extended use of food elimination diets

The first four could be seen as forms of neglect, the last two as well-intentioned but poorly executed concern.

Buying and Storing Food

If your dog suddenly balks at food that he has been happily eating and doesn't seem to be suffering any illness or problems in the mouth or throat, suspect a problem with the food. With their excellent scenting abilities, dogs can smell fats going rancid long before we humans can detect any change at all. Or the food may be contaminated with a naturally occurring grain toxin. Trust your dog's nose in these matters. Return the food or throw it out, but offer your dog a fresh choice.

To avoid having foods go rancid, moldy, or just plain stale, buy smart and store well. Purchase your food from a reliable retailer who is careful to keep stock fresh. Check the manufacturer's dating yourself. (See the end of Chapter Eight if you need help interpreting the coding.) Be sure bags or boxes are not torn or water damaged and that cans are not dented or bent.

When storing dry food at home, the most important considerations are heat and humidity. Warm moist conditions promote mold and rancidity. A cool dry environment inhibits these problems and even discourages the many tiny insects that can infest foods. If you live in, say, the steamy Southeast, store dry food in the air-conditioned portion of your home.

Other storage recommendations can be contradictory. A representative of one dog food manufacturer maintains that metal containers can cause chemical reactions with some food ingredients and recommends plastic as a nonreactive material. In contrast, literature from another manufacturer cautions against storing these foods in plastic containers, saying the plastic may react with their natural vitamin preservatives, resulting in deterioration of the food. Perhaps the best advice is to roll the bag shut and place the entire bag inside your storage container so that the food does not actually come in contact with the metal, plastic, or whatever.

Debate also concerns how tightly your containers should seal. In a humid environment, a tightly sealed container may promote condensation, certainly undesirable. But it may also keep out insects and rodents. You will have to choose based on your local conditions.

Be careful not to dump new food on top of old if you do choose to empty bags into containers. Empty and clean containers regularly.

One problem you can't overcome with proper storage is contaminants. Grains, including wheat, barley, oats, rice, and corn, may be invaded by mold under damp, humid growing conditions. The mold growing inside the closed grain head produces a toxin. The grain will not appear moldy, and processing can make the problem difficult to detect without laboratory assays.

In just such a situation in the 1990s, dogs did not reject food that was contaminated with a mycotoxin known as deoxynivalenol or, charmingly, vomatoxin. Fortunately, the effects are mild—upset stomachs, diarrhea, and vomiting—and quickly disappear once the contaminated food is removed. Once the problems were traced to the mycotoxin, the manufacturer recalled tons of dry dog food.

Undernutrition

In the 1980s, generic dog foods became popular. Their low price was certainly attractive to dog owners, but exactly what were people buying? No feeding trials were done on these foods—that's an expensive process. Instead, chemical analyses were done in a laboratory. As we have already seen, that does nothing to show that the proteins, carbohydrates, and other nutrients found in the food are in a form that the dog's digestive system can break down and use. Veterinarians began to see problems.

The foods contained a high amount of cereal fillers. The protein was found in hair and hoof material, analyzable in the lab but useless in the dog. Vitamins and minerals were at low levels. This resulted in protein/calorie deficiencies in dogs being fed these foods. They were, essentially, starving while being fed a full ration of dog food.

With problems like this, the popularity of generics was short lived. They have been replaced by store brands. These may be low priced (though not as low as the generics) or premium priced. Often, a store offers a line of products, from economy to super-premium. With retailers putting their names on the product, they are generally careful about quality. Look for a statement of feeding trials, check the list of ingredients and freshness dating, and buy with a clear conscience.

Dogs suffering a high load of internal parasites (worms) can also be protein/calorie deficient despite being fed a good quality food. Studies at the National Institute for Medical Research in England have shown that the proportion of calories derived from protein is crucial. Inadequate protein resulted in diarrhea throughout the growth stage of their test puppies. These studies also showed impaired glucose tolerance, low serum albumin, and reduced levels of vitamin A. Puppies raised on a lower protein diet (6.3 percent of calories from protein versus a control group's 12 percent) were much more susceptible to roundworm (*Toxocara canis*) infestations and slower to recover from them.

Feeding a dog table scraps or a home-cooked diet without advice of a veterinarian, or feeding a group of dogs together, can all result in protein/calorie deficiencies (with competition for food being the culprit in the group feeding scenario). The signs of this malnutrition are closely related to changes commonly seen in old age: dry, greasy, or brittle hair; abnormal shedding and lack of hair regrowth; weight loss; scaly skin; and less elastic, more pigmented skin. Note that nearly all of these signs relate to the skin and hair coat. This is no surprise when you realize that the skin can require as much as 30 percent of the daily protein intake during periods of maximum hair growth. Fortunately, dogs respond well and generally return to complete good health within three months of starting a complete and well-balanced diet.

Supplementation

People are urged to take vitamins, and many carry this thought over to their dogs, but there is a huge difference in the way we eat compared with how our dogs eat. Each day, humans select what foods to have for breakfast, lunch, dinner, and snacks. They may make good selections, resulting in appropriate servings of all the required daily nutrients, or they may choose badly and suffer a day of malnutrition. Dogs, on the other hand, generally consume one complete and balanced food day after day. Within that food are carefully balanced vitamins and minerals calculated to provide all of the dog's daily requirements.

More is *not* better in this case. Nutrients interact with one another. They cannot be considered only as single elements. Take calcium, for example. Many breeders fervently believe in calcium supplementation for their puppies. They are sure they are promoting good bone growth, fine erect ears in German Shepherd dogs, and a good start in life. Calcium is, of course, important in development of bones, joints, muscles, and teeth. No one would dispute that. However, circulating hormones such as calcitonin and parathyroid hormone, which normally regulate calcium levels in the blood, are seriously disturbed by an oversupply of calcium. Too much calcium interferes with the utilization of zinc. It can also disturb uptake of phosphorus, which is equally important in the formation of bones and teeth.

In growing puppies, oversupplementation with calcium can cause serious and possibly irreversible skeletal abnormalities. The bone growth disorders *hip dysplasia*, *wobbler syndrome*, and *hypertrophic osteodystrophy* have been linked to calcium supplementation. Excess levels of calcium also interfere with absorption of zinc, magnesium, and phosphorus, thus creating deficiencies in these minerals.

Some breeders stand by their beliefs, insisting that puppies and pregnant females require higher levels of calcium. They are correct about the higher requirements, but they neglect to take into account that these requirements are filled both by the special formulations of foods for puppies and reproducing bitches and by the increased amount of food consumed by these animals. Lowell Ackerman, DVM and

When feeding a complete and balanced dog food, vitamin and mineral supplements are unnecessary and maybe unsafe.

author of several books, maintains that the only condition requiring calcium supplementation is *eclampsia*. This occurs in bitches feeding large litters of pups. So much calcium is taken from the mother by her puppies that she simply cannot eat enough food to replace it. This is a condition requiring medical intervention—the veterinarian will give calcium intravenously.

If a dog is fed appropriate amounts of a good commercial diet yet shows signs of mineral or vitamin deficiencies, a congenital defect may be suspect. Some dog breeds—most notably Siberian Huskies and Alaskan Malamutes—are prone to zinc deficiency. They can't absorb sufficient zinc, even when fed a complete and balanced diet. Clinical signs include symmetrical crusting and scaling around the eyes and mouth, on the ears, and over the pressure points of the legs. Some nutritionists speculate that zinc deficiency was one of the major

Working Border Collies are usually lean, hard-driving dogs and may need a performance diet to maintain weight.

problems with generic dog foods, along with too much fiber. Supplementation with zinc should clear up the problem, but use supplements only under veterinary supervision. Oversupplementation can result in deficiencies of other trace minerals. Many instances of zinc deficiency are actually a result of oversupply of calcium.

A smattering of cases of abnormal metabolism of vitamin A or vitamin D have been seen at Cornell University, but this is extremely rare. These unfortunate puppies had recurring spontaneous bone fractures. Only in such extreme instances is supplementation of these vitamins appropriate. Vitamins A and D are toxic in excess amounts.

Vitamin A is also useful in another rare condition, affecting only Cocker Spaniels. In some cockers, problems of a greasy haircoat, itchy skin, and hair loss respond to supplementation with vitamin A. Again, veterinary supervision is essential.

Certain metabolic diseases—diabetes, renal disease, and hepatic

cirrhosis—can impair utilization of specific nutrients. Though this is a new topic currently under study, it appears that skin lesions seen on dogs suffering these diseases are, in fact, a result of the underlying disease. Severe crusting and cracking of the lips, pads, and hocks may occur. Supplementation with zinc, hydrolyzed amino acids, essential fatty acids, or combinations of these may produce a positive response.

In hard-working or highly stressed dogs, some supplementation may be appropriate. These dogs require extra energy. Specially formulated performance foods take that into account and supply a higher level of fat to provide the extra energy. Regular maintenance diets may be enriched to a limited extent with extra fat in the form of corn oil or lard or with a cooked egg or two, egg yolk being a good source of emulsified fatty acids. Do not use raw eggs, as they contain avidin, which binds with biotin and prevents its absorption.

Only home-cooked diets are generally lacking in calcium and possibly in trace minerals and vitamins A, D, and E. Using human foods makes formulating a diet that provides adequate canine nutrition difficult. If you are providing a home-cooked diet for a dog with food allergies or if your own philosophical beliefs lead you to choose a vegetarian diet for your canine, you will need to consult with a veterinary nutritionist to be sure that you are providing appropriate nutrition.

Risks Associated with Common Supplements

Supplement	Risks
Raw eggs	Raw egg white contains avidin, a protein that binds with the vitamin biotin and prevents its absorption. Feeding raw eggs can result in biotin deficiency or infection with salmonella.
Cod liver oil	Too much cod liver oil can supply an excess of vitamin D, which can slowly cause calcification of soft tissues and skeletal disorders.
Calcium (and other minerals)	Utilization of minerals is interwoven, and oversupply of one will result in deficiency of another. Balanced proportions are essential.
Milk	Many adult dogs cannot digest milk and will suffer gastrointestinal upset due to lactose (milk sugar) intolerance.
Vitamins	Excess water-soluble vitamins will be excreted in the dog's urine without problems, but fat-soluble vitamins in excess will be stored in muscle or fat and can reach toxic levels.
Table scraps	Limited amounts, up to no more than 10 percent of the diet, may do no harm. However, the excess calories may contribute to overnutrition and obesity (see Chapter Eleven about the problems of obese dogs).

Because supplements are nutrient dense and highly palatable, they can be helpful in cases of anorexia, coaxing dogs to eat more, and in more rapid recovery from emaciation due to disease or starvation. If you learn one thing from this section of the book, let it be that supplementation is not something to fool with on your own. See the table above for just a few of the bad results seen with inappropriate supplementation.

Preservatives, Free Radicals, and Antioxidants

Debate about preservatives in dog foods has raged on for years among dog lovers. First this, then that, preservative has been rumored to cause everything from skin rashes to reproductive failure. Are these things necessary in dog foods, and if so, are some better than others?

First, the type of food dictates the necessity of preservatives. Canned dog food is subjected to high temperatures—250 degrees and above for over an hour—so that the food is essentially sterilized. The vacuum-packing process that seals the can reduces the oxygen content to nearly zero. These two conditions prevent rancidity and render preservatives unnecessary, though a check will reveal that some canned foods do include preservatives with their fats.

Soft moist packaged foods require antimicrobial preservatives to keep them from spoiling and humectants to keep them soft. The humectants are sugars, such as corn syrup or cane molasses, and usually not the subject of much debate. However, the antimicrobials and sometimes-present antioxidants cause more concern.

Dry dog food, however, gets the most attention. Because dry food is constantly exposed to oxygen in most packaging (one company does use vacuum sealing for its dry food, and guarantees the food will remain perfectly fresh as long as the package is sealed), it is prone to oxidation and rancidity. Here, we will take a look at free radicals and antioxidants and the furor raised by some of the antioxidants/preservatives used to counteract free radical formation.

Unsaturated fats or polyunsaturated fats are named thusly because they are not saturated with hydrogen—they have space in their molecules and can react with oxygen (thus being *oxidized*) to form peroxides and hydroperoxides. As oxidation continues, new combinations are formed. Fats turn rancid. In this state, they deplete the body's reserves of vitamins A, D, E, and K and the essential fatty acids. As oxygen oxidizes fats, free radicals come into existence. Each free radical can start its own chain reaction of molecular changes. The aging process in both humans and canines is being partially blamed on the continuing process of changes generated by free radicals over the years.

So free radicals are bad. Still, we can't just leave fats out of the diet. The fatty acids from the fats are the primary building blocks of cell membranes, essential for metabolization of fat-soluble vitamins, and an important source of condensed energy. Fats are required in brain chemistry. So we include them in the diet, and we combat their oxidation with, logically, antioxidants.

However, the antioxidants them-

Is it possible that some breeds are more sensitive to preservative levels than others?

selves began to cause concern some years ago. Ethoxyquin was the first to receive a scathing report, first by a German Shepherd breeder implicating it with liver cancer, then by a Collie breeder who claimed that the chemical preservative had caused allergies, immune system problems, and reproductive failures in her dogs. Further investigation showed the Collie breeder had been feeding a commercial product imported from Canada, with ethoxyquin levels of over 200 parts per million (ppm). In U.S. manufacture, ethoxyquin at the time had a restricted use level of 150 ppm or less. Most manufacturers actually used levels of 75 to 100 ppm. Was the higher level responsible for the problems? Are lower levels safe?

To try to understand the controversy, let's examine the history of ethoxyquin. Ethoxyquin was invented (or formulated) in the 1920s and patented first in England in 1939. In the 1950s, Monsanto began exploring the possibility of using the substance as an antioxidant in animal feeds. Up to that point a crude version was being used as a rubber stabilizer (in essence, a rubber antioxidant). Now a more refined version was proposed as a feed grade antioxidant, approved by the FDA in 1956. At the same time, the FDA recognized that some amount of residue would show up in meat and poultry and saw no problem with that. You may be surprised to learn that ethoxyquin is approved for use in paprika and chili powder for human consumption. No further testing for human use was done, as Monsanto was concentrating on BHA and BHT for such uses at the time.

In 1956, Monsanto conducted a one-year study of ethoxyquin in dogs. The study found 3 milligrams of ethoxyquin per kilogram of body weight to be a safe dose and 10 milligrams per kilogram to be toxic. A narrow range between safe and toxic levels is not unusual with chemicals or even vitamins and minerals. It is important to note, however, that both the safe and toxic dosages were fed for only five days each week, not daily. This, combined with the fact that most of the problems seen at higher doses were in the liver and kidneys, raises some questions. The two days off each week would allow the liver and kidneys to regenerate somewhat. But dogs in households are fed the same food every day in most cases, so the test doesn't accurately reflect reality.

Metabolization studies were done in rats, cattle, and dogs. In rats and cattle, ethoxyquin was excreted in both the urine and feces. Dogs showed a different result. In dogs, ethoxyquin was excreted only in the urine, and 85 percent of it was not ethoxyquin itself but a metabolite of ethoxyquin (what remains after the ethoxyquin is metabolized). While this information is commonly glossed over as just more evidence of the safety of ethoxyquin, it actually seems to indicate that dogs respond differently to ethoxyquin than do some other animals commonly used in testing.

A long-term study was also undertaken, though not required for FDA approval. From 1959 through 1964, Monsanto tested ethoxyquin in a group of Beagles. Copies of this test were difficult to obtain. Monsanto claimed the test contained proprietary information and refused to release it. The FDA finally made a specific request for the test in 1987 and received a copy. After that, requests made under the Freedom of Information Act produced the report.

The study was hugely flawed. The Beagles chewed off each other's collars, making identification impossible. Even worse, they chewed through their pens, mingling the test dogs with the control dogs. There is no guarantee that the same dogs were actually fed ethoxyquin for five years. To further complicate matters, distemper hit the study hard, killing many dogs (this was before the vaccine we now all routinely use). This study would not even approach the research standards we would expect for such important issues, yet magazines and dog food manufacturers' literature report, "A five-year study found no pathological changes attributable to ethoxyquin."

Monsanto has conducted a second long-term study with ethoxyquin and dogs. While the full results have not yet been released at the time of this writing, a press release from the FDA's Center for Veterinary Medicine (CVM) will fan the flames for those concerned about ethoxyquin. The release requests a voluntary lowering of the maximum from 150 ppm to 75 ppm ethoxyquin in dog foods because "The CVM has reason to believe that the 150 ppm level may not provide an adequate margin of safety in lactating female dogs and possibly puppies." They also note that the Pet Food Institute has now undertaken a study designed to show that ethoxyquin is an effective antioxidant at levels between 30 and 60 ppm in dog food, and the CVM may request even lower levels if this study shows them to be effective.

Perhaps an additional consideration should be heightened sensitivity to ethoxyquin in some dog breeds. After all, Collies are known to be more sensitive to ivermectin, an antiheartworm drug. Maybe they also have a high sensitivity to ethoxyquin. It was a Collie breeder who helped start the whole furor!

If you are uneasy about ethoxyquin, you can choose a food that does not list the antioxidant as an added ingredient, or you can go further and select a food that guarantees its raw materials are ethoxyquin-free and tests to confirm they are. There are several available. Just keep in mind that rancidity is a valid problem, and fats in dog food must be protected against oxidation by something.

BHA (butylated hydroxyanisole) and BHT (butylated hydroxytoluene) are the other two synthetic antioxidants commonly used in dog foods. They are also used widely in foods for human consumption. (Check your bread label sometime.) Questions about their safety go back even further than the ethoxyquin controversy but have not been quite so strident nor so well reported in the dog press.

Reports show that BHA and BHT inhibit lymphocytes (the white blood cells involved in the immune response). They are also implicated in disturbing the transport and use of glucose in the body. They have been shown to induce cell proliferation in the lungs, kidneys, liver, and bladder (often a precursor to cancer).

Why are these things used at all if they have so many potential problems? We need antioxidants or our foods would go rancid or moldy. However, another choice exists—*natural* antioxidants.

Vitamin A, vitamin C, vitamin E, and beta-carotene can all protect foods, especially fats, from oxidation. Vitamin E linked with vitamin C is used most often. Dogs have no need for vitamin C (ascorbic acid) in their diet, so it doesn't matter if the vitamin C is destroyed in the process of protecting the food. Vitamin E (alpha tocopherols), however, is another story. It functions as an antioxidant by giving up an electron to a free radical, preventing a chain reaction of free radical creation. In the process, though, the vitamin E is oxidized. If conditions promoting fat oxidation are present, all of the vitamin E may be consumed. The food will then be deficient in vitamin E and rancidity will start.

Manufacturers fortify the food with enough vitamin E to both protect the ingredients and provide the dog's requirements. As long as the food is stored appropriately and sold promptly, the vitamin will serve both functions well.

If you are concerned about preservatives, vitamin E (usually identified as *mixed tocopherols*) is your obvious choice. It actually has beneficial rather than detrimental side effects. Just be sure to check the package dating and store the food carefully. Its shelf life is markedly shorter. Veterinarian nutritionists recommend use within 30 or 60 days of manufacture to ensure that the fats are protected from rancidity. David Dzanis of the FDA notes that dog food companies have reported more complaints about off odors and rancidity problems in foods with tocopherols as the preservatives. They are definitely not as powerful an antioxidant as the more artificial and more controversial ethoxyquin, BHA, and BHT.

It *IS* a Business, After All

An animal welfare organization has put out an investigative report very critical of dog food and dog food manufacturers. They point out that four of the five major U.S. pet food companies are subsidiaries of huge multinational food companies, giving them a "captive market in which to dump their waste products."

Well, as the heading for this section says, the manufacturing of dog food *is* a business. Companies are in business to make a profit, no matter what the final product. Consumers should know that as a simple fact of life. Manufacturers are also well aware that any product not living up to its promise will be rejected by consumers. Yet consumers demand low, or at least reasonable, cost and high quality. It is a delicate dance between producer and consumer, cost and quality. Marrying compatible industries under one company is one way of helping to lower cost. But concentrating on convenience and profit at the expense of quality would certainly be detrimental to dogs.

As with all issues, there are rarely absolutes, no cut-and-dried, black-and-white heroes and villains.

This investigative report goes on to say that pet foods are inedible scraps fortified with vitamins and minerals, preserved to sit on a shelf for over a year, with dyes added to make it pretty, cut into fancy shapes. Does this sound like breakfast cereal to anyone?

If pet foods were indeed made of inedible scraps, dogs wouldn't survive for long on them, even if they were fortified with vitamins and minerals. The necessary nutrients simply wouldn't be there. As to preservatives and dyes, yes, dog foods contain them but so do the majority of foods for human consumption found on the supermarket shelves. If we want to change that, we have to work on our own diets first.

The report does make some reasonable points as well. In discussing the animal fats commonly sprayed onto dry foods, it points out that those fats may come from supermarket trimmings from the packaging of meats, packinghouse wastes, or restaurant grease. Well, fat from supermarket trimmings was deemed fit for human consumption, so no problem there. Packinghouse wastes can cover a wide range of high- to low-quality scraps. Restaurant grease—often stored in 50-gallon drums outdoors in the sun for days or weeks—is a low-quality ingredient. The label will not tell you just where the animal fats in the food come from. You will have to ask the manufacturer.

When the report says soy is a common ingredient in many pet foods and most popular brands of pet food today use a variable formula diet, you know they're investigating economy or premium foods. Super-premium foods, according to the definition developed by *Good Dog!* magazine, do not include soy. Variable formula diets—where the content of the food can change from batch to batch depending on the prices of the ingredients—are also not used in super-premium foods. They produce fixed formula diets, using the same ingredients for each batch.

Remember, it is a business. The pet food manufacturers charging

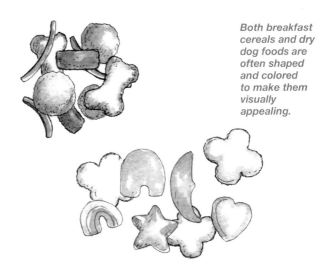

Both breakfast cereals and dry dog foods are often shaped and colored to make them visually appealing.

more for their super-premium foods need to deliver a product that performs better than its cheaper competitors or lose their customers.

Rendered Pets

Every so often a headline blares something like, "How Dogs and Cats Get Recycled into Pet Food." (That example is actually from the February 20, 1990 edition of the *San Francisco Chronicle*.) Emotions tend to run high on this topic. Somehow, the idea of pets eating other pets is abhorrent. Cannibalism doesn't seem any more appropriate for our pets than for ourselves.

So does it happen? Pet food manufacturers all say no. The risk of bad publicity far outweighs any conceivable benefit (and it's hard to imagine what the benefits would be). They demand assurance from

It is highly unlikely that any rendered pets end up as ingredients in dog foods.

Though the practice is less prevalent now than in the past, some shelters still do sell the remains to an independent renderer.

The few independent renderers accepting this material value the large-volume business of the pet food manufacturers and are well aware of their ban on processed companion animals. Both sides insist that this ingredient does not find its way into pet foods. David Dzanis of the FDA's Center for Veterinary Medicine states, "They are used for fertilizers and industrial lubricants, which is appalling enough in its own way. Companies using bone meal can specify what materials they want in there."

In an interesting side note, these remains are sometimes sold to large poultry-raising operations. (Bet you didn't think of chickens as carnivores!) So in a roundabout, up-the-food-chain sort of way, dog food could conceivably include poultry that was fed rendered companion animals. In fact, this poultry could just as easily end up in the meat counter and on your plate.

An investigation of the poultry-raising operations is a whole separate issue and one that animal welfare organizations could look into with potential benefits for us all. If you find the prospect of your pet eating food including chickens that have eaten rendered pets too horrible, your only sure solution is to choose a food that does not include poultry products. However, read the next section before making that decision.

their animal protein and fat suppliers that no processed dead companion animals are included in their blends.

Several sorts of renderers exist. Poultry processors deal only with poultry by-products. Packer renderers are involved in the slaughter of food animals and render only whatever type of animal they are slaughtering. Neither of these will deal with any sort of companion animals.

Independent renderers, the most abundant variety in the United States, get their raw materials from supermarkets, small packing houses, and other sources. It's those other sources that become the issue.

Animal shelters, faced with the sad task of euthanizing unwanted cats and dogs, have to dispose of the remains in a sanitary manner.

Don't Have a (Mad) Cow, Man

Mad cow disease crashed into the public consciousness in 1996 and 1997. A British outbreak of the disease more properly called bovine spongiform encephalopathy (BSE) made headlines around the world. A mysterious disease, it actually eats holes in the brain of the afflicted creature. In humans, it's called Jakob-Creutzfeldt Disease.

Contrary to the impression given by media coverage, this is not a new problem. In the 1950s, sheep were the affected species, and the disease was called scrapie. Serious outbreaks occurred in the United States, Australia, and New Zealand. In Australia and New Zealand, where sheep outnumber people, the reaction was swift and serious. Wherever infected sheep were found, entire flocks were killed. The drastic action apparently wiped out the disease. New Zealand and Australia have been scrapie-free ever since, and most of the pet food companies making lamb and rice diets buy their lamb from these countries for that reason.

In the United States, scrapie still exists, though it is not a prevalent problem. No cases of BSE have been seen within U.S. borders. However, Jakob-Creutzfeldt Disease is here, and scientists are making some unsettling discoveries about it. The disease is not at all well understood. It is not caused by a virus or a bacteria but by a strange type of protein, and thus is not alive, which means it can't be killed. It was thought that high heat inactivated it, and thus sterilization of medical instruments was a safety guarantee. This has now been called into question.

The disease is definitely passed by eating brains or spinal cords containing the rogue protein. It can also be passed by blood. Several of the British human fatalities are blamed on contact of an open wound with contaminated beef. The possibility of transmission through blood donation is a chilling one.

Hormones are another possible problem area. It is gruesome enough that many fertility and growth hormones are derived from corpses, but now the spectre of a brain-eating protein arises. Six deaths in Australia were tentatively traced to hormone injections.

Mad sheep disease (scrapie) has actually been an acknowledged problem longer than mad cow disease.

In Britain, the condition has been passed to cats and unimaginatively dubbed mad cat disease. From 1990 to 1996, 70 cats are known to have died from their own form of spongiform encephalopathy. The thinking now is that the cat food they were eating contained cattle suffering from BSE. These were also older cats, who may have become infected before any actions were taken to prevent transmission. British spokespeople point out that this occurred in 70 cats out of a cat population exceeding seven million.

No dogs anywhere in the world have been definitively diagnosed with a form of spongiform encephalopathy. No one knows if they are somehow immune or merely incredibly lucky so far. If you have concerns nonetheless, you can look for a poultry-based food. Chickens, turkeys, and other birds are not affected by this brain condition.

One canine case caused a flurry, as it was the first suspected instance of spongiform encephalopathy in dogs. An 11-year-old Labrador Retriever in Norway with seizures and lack of muscular coordination was found by postmortem to have brain lesions similar to mad cow disease. Sections of the brain were sent to researchers in Britain to determine whether or not this is indeed the first case of canine spongiform encephalopathy. But Ivan Burger at the Waltham Centre for Pet Nutrition reported that it has proven to be due to another cause, not BSE.

Countries have moved swiftly to counteract the danger of BSE. New regulations in the United States prohibit any mammalian tissues in feeds for ruminants. Britain has gone further and banned the feeding of mammalian protein to ALL food animals, including swine and poultry.

Points
to Remember

- Ingredients are not necessarily an indication of quality.
- Ingredients that human consumers find unappealing could be nutritionally preferable to ingredients with greater consumer appeal.
- No reference to quality of ingredients is permitted on dog food packaging.
- If a healthy dog suddenly rejects a food, suspect a problem with the food—the dog may be detecting early rancidity or a toxin of some kind. Provide fresh food.
- Always check package dating to be sure you are purchasing a fresh product, and store it carefully.
- Generic dog foods have been shown to be the culprit in cases of malnutrition.
- Supplementation, especially with calcium or phosphorus, should never be undertaken without the advice of a veterinarian.
- Congenital defects, many of them known to occur in specific breeds, may be the cause of vitamin or mineral deficiencies.
- Preservatives are necessary, particularly in dry foods, to ensure that fats do not go rancid.
- Controversy over the safety of ethoxyquin, BHA, and BHT has led many manufacturers to switch to natural preservatives such as vitamin E. Foods relying on natural preservatives are protected for a considerably shorter time.
- Foods relying on vitamin E for preservation must provide enough of the vitamin to both protect the food and satisfy the dog's requirement for the vitamin.
- Dog food manufacturers are in business to make money, and you must realize this as a fact of life.
- Rendered pets ending up in pet food is a rare occurrence, denied by pet food manufacturers and renderers alike.
- Mad cow disease is only the latest of a variety of outbreaks of spongiform encephalopathy—scrapie in sheep, Jakob-Creutzfeldt in humans.

Chapter Eight
Digging Into Dog Food

In supermarkets, where shelf space is fought over with ferocious abandon, dog food occupies as much as one entire aisle. Pet supply superstores may devote three, four, or more aisles to dog food alone. More than $8 billion worth of pet food is sold in the United States each year by over 100 pet food manufacturers.

You can discuss dog foods with shopkeepers, who may get feedback from their customers.

So many brands, so many types, so many flavors, so many claims . . . canned food, semimoist food, flaked food, kibbled food . . . how is the poor dog owner to choose?

Just as in food for human consumption, labels can offer a great deal of valuable information (though the regulations for labeling human foods and pet foods differ greatly). The label is a legal document meant to communicate the contents of the package. You just have to know how to read it.

What the Label Will Tell You

Regulatory Agencies

Pet food labels must meet criteria established by the Food and Drug Administration (FDA), the U.S. Department of Agriculture (USDA), the Federal Trade Commission (FTC), and state requirements mostly based on the Association of American Feed Control Officials (AAFCO) guidelines. The Pet Food Institute also has a voluntary hand in the information found on labels, with its Nutrition Assurance Program.

Until the 1980s, the National Research Council (NRC) determined the minimum nutritional requirements for pets. However, in 1992, the Council declared that it no longer wanted to develop these guidelines and passed the responsibility along to AAFCO.

AAFCO commissioned a canine nutrition expert subcommittee composed of research and industry authorities to set up nutrient profiles for dogs. The resulting work, *AAFCO Nutrient Profiles for Dog Foods*, was published in 1992. For the first time, guidelines included not just minimum recommended levels but maximum levels as well for nutrients such as calcium, phosphorus, iron, zinc, and fat-soluble vitamins. The new guidelines also provided specific amino acid requirements to ensure quality protein, and increased the requirements for iron, zinc, and fat for growing or reproducing dogs.

However, AAFCO is not an official regulatory entity. It is only an advisory body, composed of members from each of the states, with a goal of making state regulations consistent. Each state actually has its own feed regulation and registration requirements. Many are based on AAFCO's model, but some are not.

The USDA oversees the processing of animal products and cereal grains for pets just as it does for humans. The FDA approves artificial preservatives, colorings, and flavorings and also passes judgment on product labeling and any health claims made for a specific food. The FTC oversees advertising, including radio, TV, print, and even statements made by companies' salespersons.

In Europe, legislation covering *animal feeding stuffs* originates primarily in European Community directives. These are then implemented through national regulations, such as England's Feeding Stuffs Regulations. Industry trade associations, like the Pet Food Manufacturer's Association, are also found in Great Britain.

These many agencies together dictate what must, can, and cannot appear on pet food labels.

Main Display Panel

The front main display panel of a bag, box, or can of dog food will reveal the less-than-astonishing information that this is indeed dog food. There must also be a statement indicating how much food is included in the package (net weight). This can be helpful in comparing prices, but not as much as you may think, because we have no indication of quality.

A couple of pieces of truly useful information *are* to be found on display panels, however. The first is the flavor of the food. Wording is very strictly regulated here, and the glossary will explain what *flavor* and other such descriptive words actually mean. For now, realize that the statement "beef flavor" on a label does not mean the food has to contain any actual beef. What may look like beefy chunks in the food itself may be textured vegetable protein.

The second piece of information is a nutrition statement regarding what life stage the food is meant to satisfy. How the information was verified will be found on the information panel.

On some foods, you may see a claim that it "meets or exceeds the nutritional requirements for all life stages of your dog." Understand that a food that meets the needs of growing puppies will definitely exceed the needs of the average adult dog. Unless you feed far less of the food, you will likely end up with an obese dog in short measure. Scientific evidence has also shown that the dog's nutritional needs change throughout its life, and no one food can optimally meet those varying needs. Look instead for a statement that the food is for either growth (puppies), maintenance (adults), reproduction (pregnant or nursing females), senior, or possibly performance (hard-working adults).

Two other statements might be found. On snacks or treats, not meant as the sole sustenance for a dog, you will find "not to be fed as the total diet." Special-purpose products developed for use with diseases or other maladies may state "Use only as directed by your veterinarian." They must also carry the regular AAFCO life stage feeding substantiation statement or state "intermittent or supplemental feeding only."

Other, optional bits of information may appear on the main display panel. Comparative claims can be made, so long as they're truthful. The same is true for negative claims, such as "free from preservatives" or "no soy." The word *natural* must be combined with a disclaimer such as "natural ingredients plus essential vitamins and minerals." The food labeled this way cannot contain any artificial colors, flavors, or preservatives.

Any photographs of food items shown on the label must reflect the actual contents of the food. A product using poultry meal cannot picture a nice plump whole chicken on the label. This would be considered misleading.

Another option is *bursts*, those promotional statements often appearing in colorful banners or stars. They may say such things as, "Complete and balanced," or "100% nutritionally complete," and are supposed to be verifiable.

An increasingly popular label is *light* (or *lean*, or *lite*, or *reduced*). In the past, regulations have required only that the product for which the claim is being made contain at least 15 percent lower energy (lite) or fat (lean) than *the product to which it is being compared*. Under this definition, one company's light food could actually contain *more* calories than another company's regular product. Under the newest regulations, foods labeled light, low calorie, or similar terms may contain no more than 3,100 kcal ME/kg for products containing less than 20 percent moisture (dry foods), 2,500 kcal ME/kg for products with moisture between 20 and 65 percent (semimoist foods), and no more than 900 kcal ME/kg for products with moisture over 65 percent (canned foods). The label must bear a calorie content statement.

The terms *less calories* or *reduced calories* have their own regulations. The product being used for comparison must be stated, and the percentage of reduction in calories must be given.

The terms *lean* or *low fat* mean that the food must contain no more than 9 percent crude fat for products with moisture content of less than 20 percent, no more than 7 percent for products with 20 to 65 percent moisture, and no more than 4 percent crude fat for products containing more than 65 percent moisture. The label must bear a maximum crude fat guarantee immediately following the minimum crude fat guarantee.

Finally, the terms *less* or *reduced fat* require that the label state the product of comparison and the percentage of fat reduction. This label also must bear a maximum crude fat guarantee.

Any specific health claims, such as "reduces tartar" or "helps maintain urinary tract health" must be reviewed by the Food and Drug Administration. No official guide-

lines exist, however, for words like *premium*, *gourmet*, or *ultimate* or the statement "recommended by veterinarians."

Information Panel

This is where an abundance of hard-core information waits to be found, if only you can understand it. The two biggest chunks of information that must be included are the guaranteed analysis and the list of ingredients. These can be confusing. Take a deep breath and read on—this is as dog owner-friendly as possible.

Look first for a statement that the food was tested in feeding trials per AAFCO guidelines.

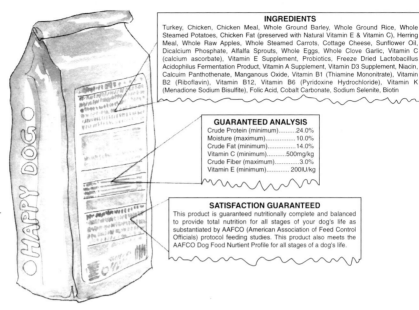

INGREDIENTS

Turkey, Chicken, Chicken Meal, Whole Ground Barley, Whole Ground Rice, Whole Steamed Potatoes, Chicken Fat (preserved with Natural Vitamin E & Vitamin C), Herring Meal, Whole Raw Apples, Whole Steamed Carrots, Cottage Cheese, Sunflower Oil, Dicalcium Phosphate, Alfalfa Sprouts, Whole Eggs, Whole Clove Garlic, Vitamin C (calcium ascorbate), Vitamin E Supplement, Probiotics, Freeze Dried Lactobacillus Acidophilus Fermentation Product, Vitamin A Supplement, Vitamin D3 Supplement, Niacin, Calcuim Panthothenate, Manganous Oxide, Vitamin B1 (Thiamine Mononitrate), Vitamin B2 (Riboflavin), Vitamin B12, Vitamin B6 (Pyridoxine Hydrochloride), Vitamin K (Menadione Sodium Bisulfite), Folic Acid, Cobalt Carbonate, Sodium Selenite, Biotin

GUARANTEED ANALYSIS

Crude Protein (minimum)..........24.0%
Moisture (maximum)................10.0%
Crude Fat (minimum)...............14.0%
Vitamin C (minimum)...........500mg/kg
Crude Fiber (maximum).............3.0%
Vitamin E (minimum)............ 200IU/kg

SATISFACTION GUARANTEED

This product is guaranteed nutritionally complete and balanced to provide total nutrition for all stages of your dog's life as substantiated by AAFCO (American Association of Feed Control Officials) protocol feeding studies. This product also meets the AAFCO Dog Food Nurtient Profile for all stages of a dog's life.

The guaranteed analysis looks very scientific and reassuring with its list of nutrients and the quantities or percentages of each included in the food. However, the only actual guarantee is that the named nutrient is present in the food in some amount. While the uncertainty has decreased somewhat since AAFCO started using guidelines for maximum as well as minimum percentages, differences in moisture content can cause big differences in the presence of nutrients. Maximums may be set high to allow for spikes in the content of some nutrient because a food tested and found exceeding the percentages stated on the package will be declared *misbranded* and must be discarded. No manufacturer wants that! Also, the AAFCO guidelines are given on a dry matter basis, while most val-ues on dog food labels are cited *as fed* (as required by regulation).

A dry matter analysis eliminates the uncertainties of moisture content and allows you to compare nutrient amounts with AAFCO guidelines. Unfortunately, this information is not required on the label, but it is almost always included in manufacturer's literature. Pet food stores will sometimes have racks of food samples and accompanying literature. If you cannot find such a display, you can check the product packaging for a toll-free telephone number and call the manufacturer to request information or literature. The telephone number is not required information, but many companies include it nonetheless.

Call the manufacturer and ask for the actual nutritional analysis. This will both provide you with more helpful numbers for comparison and indicate the manufacturer's willingness to provide consumers with information. If no phone number is provided, you will have to go the longer route of writing to request information—an address is required. Another option is to watch your local pet supply store for events where food representatives staff booths and can be approached directly.

Ask for the digestibility of the food. It should be at least 75 percent. Compare the numbers the manufacturer has given you with the AAFCO guidelines (shown in Chapter Five).

Reading the ingredients lists of the foods you eat is probably a confusing experience. Reading dog food labels will not be any improvement. There are more than 600 potential ingredients defined by AAFCO, many with arcane or misleading names.

Ingredients are listed by weight, with the most predominant ingredient listed first and on down the line. However, this can be very deceiving. The label does not indicate whether dry weights or moisture-included weights are being used, and some ingredients may be listed one way and some the other. *Dressed chicken* or simply *chicken* appearing first in a list may sound very appealing. However, the reason it stands first in line is that dressed chicken is a high-moisture product, and 70 percent of that weight is actually water.

Another bit of subterfuge used by some manufacturers is *splitting*, listing a single type of ingredient by a variety of names to keep it from appearing too high on the list. If you added listings of corn gluten, ground corn, corn syrup, and corn germ meal together, corn might become the first ingredient listed rather than that water-heavy dressed chicken. But not all splitting is done to hide and confuse ingredients. If a manufacturer of a canned food wants to use rice flour as a binding agent to give the food a good consistency, but include whole rice to make the food more visually appealing, that's a legitimate reason to split ingredients. Why a manufacturer is splitting ingredients is not always readily apparent.

Also, the quality of an ingredient is not obvious simply from its name. Good, highly nutritious poultry by-product meal and nearly indigestible, nutritionally useless poultry by-product meal both exist. The name will not tell you which is which.

One pet food manufacturer suggests that an animal protein source should be one of the first two listed ingredients in a canned food or the first three in a dry food. There should also be at least one cereal grain and one source of calcium.

No reference to the *quality* of ingredients is permitted on labeling. Any advertising touting one nutrient, such as protein, as more beneficial than others should be ignored. All nutrients should be provided in balanced, digestible amounts suitable to the dog's requirements as determined by life stage, metabolism, and environment.

The glossary will help you decipher some of the more esoteric ingredient names. Labeling terms are very specific and are often chosen to sound good to the dog food purchaser. Keep in mind that different grades of ingredient quality can be within the same AAFCO-regulated definition.

The information panel is also where you will find the method used to substantiate the life stage statement. The life stage statement comes in two different forms. The sentence, "This product is formulated (or calculated) to meet the AAFCO dog food nutrient profile for [whatever life stage]" means a laboratory chemical analysis was done on the food. Think about this. With the formulation method, some laboratory took a sample of dog food and did tests to show that the food contained a certain amount of crude protein, some other amount of crude fiber, and so on. The word *crude* itself refers to an amount measured by laboratory equipment, *not* the amount that can actually be used by the dog.

Hill's Science Diet once concocted a "diet" consisting of some old leather shoes, used crank case oil, and other such less-than-delectable items of nonfood. Under laboratory analysis, this "diet" provided the required minimum amounts of crude protein, fat, and fiber and could have been labeled as meeting the NRC guidelines being used at the time.

The calculation method is even worse. It simply adds up all the nutrients in each of the ingredients (still with no assurance that they are actu-

ally usable by the dog) and compares the total to the AAFCO profile.

Much more desirable is the statement, "Animal feeding tests using AAFCO procedures substantiate that [product name] provides complete and balanced nutrition for [whatever life stage]." This means the product has been tested by actually feeding it to real dogs. The regulations for such trials will be discussed later in this chapter.

Other Label Information

If the dog food is sold as *complete and balanced*, feeding guidelines must be included on the label. These should always be considered as only guidelines. The actual amount required by your dog will depend on age, size, activity, environment, and metabolism. A typical label on a canned food might tell you to feed a medium-sized dog between three-quarters and one and one-half cans. This is a huge variance, with about a 500-calorie difference between the low and high ends. If you fed the maximum recommended amount to a dog who required only the minimum recommended amount, you would have a seriously obese dog very quickly.

As previously noted, the manufacturer's or distributor's name and address must be included on the label. The notation *manufactured by* means that the named company actually makes its own food and is responsible for its own quality control. *Manufactured for* or *distributed by* indicates that another company actually manufactures the food.

Since 1994, calorie claims have been allowed on pet food labels. If included, they are stated as "Metabolizable energy: kilocalories per kilogram (kcal/kg)," and may also be stated as kilocalories per some measure such as a cup or can. The calories per unit of food will be one of the biggest differences between dog foods.

What the Label Won't Tell You

Though it may give some hints, the label will not tell you the quality of a dog food. You can look for a statement that feeding trials were conducted in accordance with AAFCO guidelines, even that they included palatability and digestibility studies. You can read any promotional statements the manufacturer makes about itself or its food. You can compare prices. It's more expensive to conduct feeding trials and use higher-quality ingredients, and those costs are reflected in the price of the food. When it comes to dog food, you do, at least to some extent, get what you pay for.

You may come across the terms *premium*, *super-premium*, and *economy* or *regular*. These are broad categories, each encompassing a variety of foods, and their definitions are not regulated. In fact, the magazine *Good Dog!* originated use of the terms.

Generally, some store brands or other low-cost foods are termed *regular*. To offer low prices, less-expensive ingredients are used. Advertising is generally nil. With generics, costly feeding trials aren't performed and nutrition is doubtful, but store brands usually do hire testing laboratories to conduct feeding trials. Economy foods may not be very palatable.

The distinction between premium and super-premium is more difficult. All are likely to be nationally recognized brands. Some people consider brands sold in supermarkets to be of lower quality than those sold only in pet supply stores, feed stores, or even veterinarians' offices. That's not necessarily the case.

Super-premium foods can be nebulously defined only as those offered by manufacturers with an extensive background of research in canine nutrition, which have undergone feeding trials and palatability and digestibility testing, offer a high level of nutrient density, and maintain

Before you read ingredients, know what you're looking for.

of combinations—dog food must be complete and balanced, able to provide everything the dog needs in the correct amounts. (Some veterinarians and even pet food manufacturers maintain that this goal cannot possibly be attained. They make recommendations such as adding fresh foods to commercial diets, adding supplements to commercial diets, or feeding whole raw foods instead of a commercial diet. This will be discussed further in Chapter Eleven.)

For the nutrients to be of any use, the food must be palatable (so the dog will eat enough of it) and digestible (so the nutrients will be utilized by the dog's body systems).

Feeding trials test all of these aspects. But first a proposed product has to show significant promise to be worth the expense.

A new manufacturing technique, a nutritional improvement, or simply market research can generate a proposed new product. Before any product is actually made, the idea is presented to consumers in small focus groups and then bigger groups. If the idea shows promise, it is then made into a prototype product and used in feeding trials.

Companies developing new products have a great deal to consider. They are actually working to satisfy two customers—the dog, of course, but also the dog owner who makes the food purchase. So dog food must first appeal to dog owners. This can impact the manufacturer's bottom line, a consideration very important to the manufacturer. How-

quality manufacturing controls and quality assurance. Super-premium foods definitely do not include soy. Some labels will provide more information on these topics than others.

Feeding Trials

You've been reading about feeding trials throughout this chapter. It's time we looked at exactly what they are and how they work.

Dogs consume five basic nutrient groups—proteins, carbohydrates, fats, minerals, and vitamins. You can also look at this as consumption of four basic food groups—meat and fish, dairy and eggs, cereals and vegetables, and fats and oils. Plus water. No nutrient can be considered in isolation, because their biochemical interactions are incredibly complex. Since dogs are usually fed one or maybe two foods as their total diet—unlike our own ever-changing menu

ever, the quality of the food is a matter of life and death for the dog.

In developing a complete and balanced diet, a manufacturer must consider nutrient content, energy content, digestibility, palatability, and the all-important balance of nutrients. Even the most wonderfully developed food, one with an ideal nutrient profile and delectable palatability, is of no use if it can't be broken down and assimilated by the dog. So, feeding trials are conducted.

Foods intended for different life stages obviously have different requirements. The AAFCO guidelines for an adult (maintenance) feeding trial specify at least eight adult dogs of either sex and any size. These dogs will be fed only the test diet and water for at least 26 weeks. Researchers track the daily food intake of each dog, keep records of body weight, perform physical examinations and blood chemistry profiles, and note any unusual factors such as a change in health. At the end of the trial, the dogs must have maintained their original body condition, with no significant variations in body weight, and must have shown no abnormal problems that might be diet related. Weight loss of more than 15 percent individually or 10 percent as a group constitutes a test failure. (Critics contend that the group is not large enough and the time span not long enough to generate any conclusive results.)

Other feeding trials are more specific in their requirements. Reproduction study guidelines specify two

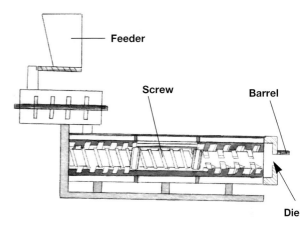

groups of females, at least eight in each group. The study females must be the same breed, at least one year old, and in at least their second heat period. They are all housed under the same conditions, fed at the same time from the same size bowls. One group is fed the test diet while the other group is fed a control food of proven quality.

The test begins before the bitches are bred and continues until the puppies reach seven to eight weeks of age. Because not all bitches come into season at precisely the same time, the duration of the test period will vary. Observations include the daily food intake of each mother and each puppy (once the puppies are eating solid food in addition to nursing), the weekly body weight of the mothers, and the birth weights and then weekly weights of the puppies. The number and sex of the puppies born and weaned by each bitch are recorded. Blood chemistry profiles are performed on the mothers, and any

The development of the extrusion process—where the mixture of dog food ingredients is moved by the rotating screw to the die and cut to shape and size—was responsible for an array of new dog foods.

unusual factors in either the mothers or the pups are noted. Complete physical exams are performed on the mothers and puppies. The new food must perform better than or at least as well as the control food or improve on historical data for the test group.

The puppies from the reproduction study are often moved from there directly to a growth study. The pups are divided, by sex and weight, as equally as possible into two groups, with at least eight puppies in each group. One group is fed the test diet while the other is fed a proven control. The testing begins when the puppies are seven to eight weeks of age and continues for at least ten weeks. Observations are much the same as in the other studies, including daily food intake, weekly body weight, physical exams, blood chemistry profiles, and a lookout for any unusual factors.

If one test food passes both the reproduction study and the growth study it can, by law, be labeled as "complete and balanced nutrition for all life stages." One food can satisfy the similar nutritional needs of puppies and pregnant or nursing females, especially if fed free choice. However, this same food would need to be fed under strict quantity instructions to avoid providing more nutrition (calories) and higher levels of particular nutrients than a nonreproducing adult dog would require. Taking into account owners' predilection to overfeed, such a dog would gain too much weight on this diet. Normal adults simply do not require as high a level per pound of body weight of protein, energy, vitamins, or minerals. In fact, they require about half the nutrient intake per pound of body weight as they did while growing.

While the feeding trials are being conducted, the manufacturer is not idle. Product name and package design are being developed. Consumer research is continuing. If any new equipment will be required for manufacture of the product or packaging, it is probably being designed.

Palatability and Digestibility Studies

Many manufacturers also conduct palatability studies and digestion studies. However, neither is currently required by law.

In palatability tests, each dog is offered two foods. The foods are presented in the same size bowls, each containing more than the dog can eat. To ensure that there is no left/right bias—some dogs favor one side over the other—the position of the bowls is switched daily. Observers simply note how much of each food the dog eats and then chart the preferences. A new product may be subject to palatability testing for up to one year to check for any changes due to storage.

Contrary to public opinion, dogs are actually discriminating diners. Their finely tuned noses and well-developed taste buds can easily detect differences in the quality of ingredients making up a dog food. Overcooked or scorched ingredients are not appealing, and spoiled or rancid foods are certainly not going to contribute to good taste. Foods with such ingredients may be eaten reluctantly or rejected completely.

Something termed *mouth feel* is also important to canine consumers. You might have thought those different little dog food shapes were meant to appeal only to you, but actually, dogs favor different shapes and sizes of food over others. Texture and density are also important. All of these factors enter into palatability.

AAFCO has protocols for digestion studies, but such studies are not required. Various companies develop their own procedures. This can make comparing foods difficult. However, all digestion studies attempt to quantify first the nutrients in a food and, second, the nutrients actually available to the animal metabolically.

The study dogs are fed only the test food. After a few days allowed for the dogs' metabolism to adjust to the food, the collection period begins. The total amount of food consumed and total amount of fecal material are tracked for each dog. Nutritional analyses of the food and the fecal material are performed. The digestibility for each nutrient is calculated by subtracting the amount of the nutrient found in the stool from the total amount of the nutrient that the dog consumed in the food. Digestibility on a dry matter basis should be at least 75 percent.

Product Freshness Dating

Four methods are generally used to date packages. The international date code consists of two numbers for the day of the month, two numbers for the month, and two numbers for the year, as follows:

270598 = the 27th day of
the 5th month in 1998,
or May 27, 1998.

Julian calendar dating counts the days of the year from start to finish— 1 to 365 or 366—and the last two numbers or sometimes only the last one number of the year. So the code

Reproduction is very demanding for the mother. Food must provide sufficient nutrition for her needs and for the milk for her puppies.

Mouth feel is one reason that dog foods come in different sizes and shapes.

0459 or 04599 means the 45th day of the year 1999, or February 14, 1999.

Pretty obvious is the month/day/year system of dating. It appears much as the date you might write in your checkbook, without the slashes: 093098, or September 30, 1998.

Best before uses the month/day/year format to indicate the date by which the product should be eaten. So 06/05/99 means use up this food by early June. The manufacturer calculates the shelf life, including a margin of safety. The food may have been manufactured anywhere from six to 12 months prior to that date.

A few foods use dating schemes all their own. Cycle, for example, has a coding sequence with the last number of the year followed by a letter plant code, then the day, then a letter code for the month, then numbers representing the shift and the hour the bag or can was produced. This looks like 8P27H25, which translates to August 27, 1998 (the H represents the eighth letter and thus the eighth month).

Understanding freshness dating is important, especially if you choose a food preserved with natural preservatives such as mixed tocopherols. While these preservatives are fine, they do not protect for as long as the synthetic preservatives BHA, BHT, and ethoxyquin do.

Points to Remember

- The label is a legal document, meant to satisfy legal requirements, not the inquiries of consumers.
- Look for a product with the statement that "animal feeding tests using AAFCO procedures" have been performed.
- The guaranteed analysis is only a rough indication of product nutrients at best. Getting a dry matter analysis and digestibility percentage from the manufacturer is much more indicative of quality.
- Ingredients are listed by weight, but some are dry weights and some are moisture-added weights.

- Splitting can be used to keep certain ingredients lower down the list.
- Feeding guidelines should always be considered as only rough guidelines.
- Nutrients in food are of no use unless they can be metabolized by the animal eating the food.
- Product freshness dating is important and should always be checked.
- Your surest guide to a good-quality food is the reputation of the manufacturer, AAFCO feeding trials, the quality of ingredients as indicated by the list of ingredients and the cost of the food, and your own dog's health and well-being while consuming the food.

Chapter Nine

One Dog, One Food?

Some dog foods out there claim they are complete and balanced for all stages of life. Can this be correct? Can you really feed your ten-week-old puppy and ten-year-old senior the same food and have them both prosper?

Years ago, people would have thought you crazy for asking such a question. Dog food was dog food. There were no life stages. If you bothered to buy dog food at all, you either stuck to one product with great loyalty or bought whatever was on sale.

Puppy foods were the first specialty formulations to come along. It wasn't much of a stretch to realize that rapidly growing puppies might need different or at least higher levels of nutrients than adults. Many dog owners were willing to spend a little more on puppies to ensure proper nutrition for them. Now, puppy foods are even breaking down into sub-classes of large and small puppies. And if puppies need special foods, what about their mothers?

Overweight dogs were the next subpopulation to receive attention. If puppies needed more nutrients, pudgies needed less. Weight-reduction formulations were soon available. This large subject is discussed in the next chapter.

Supper for seniors is still a hot topic with dog food companies. Foods for seniors have been available for years, but formulations are changing based on continuing research. Even the question of when a dog is a senior is a matter for debate.

Finally, high-performance foods are available for hard-working dogs. This is certainly a smaller group than puppies or seniors but one with its own nutritional needs.

So how can an all-stage food satisfy these varying needs? Actually, it meets the highest levels of nutrients required, say for a puppy or a nursing mother. It can then legally say it is complete for all life stages, ignoring the fact that it provides excess nutrients to the other, less-demanding life stages. Feeding the same food to every dog regardless of age, activity, or health may seem convenient, and many dogs may even do reasonably well on such a feeding plan. However, you can do better.

Good nutrition means a shiny coat, a lean, well-muscled body, and plenty of energy, as demonstrated by this Jack Russell Terrier.

In this chapter, we will examine the special needs of and special foods for puppies, pregnant and nursing mothers, seniors, and working dogs. (Remember, Chapter Ten discusses overweight or inactive dogs and foods for them.)

Puppies and Young Adults

For their first few weeks (and, really, even before they are born), puppies' nutrition is based on what you feed their mother. While puppies are nursing, they develop food preferences, strange as that may sound. The mother's milk is flavored by the food she consumes, and puppies take strong cues from those flavors.

At three or four weeks of age, the puppies start to show some interest in solid foods and can begin learning to eat from a bowl. The food they are offered should be highly palatable and nutrient dense. Soft wet foods may be more appealing and easier for puppies to eat (and more fun for them to play in), but small kibbles softened with liquid will also work. Do not use cow's milk, as dogs generally lack the enzyme necessary to break down cow's milk protein. Water, goat's milk, or yogurt are all good choices.

Be careful that the food you select to feed your puppy has a variety of ingredients. A study showed that puppies fed a soybean diet would later accept no other foods. Those fed a vegetarian diet of mixed sources would eat other grains and vegetables but would not accept meat. Those who consumed a diet of meats, grains, and vegetables would eat any new food unless it tasted bitter, sour, or stale. Limited early experience leads to limited food acceptance.

While they are nursing, puppies should gain approximately their birth weight each week. Put another way, nursing puppies should be expected to gain one or two grams each day for every pound of expected adult weight. Does this still hold true once they start being fed by you rather than their mother? Consult the following table of energy requirements.

Energy Requirements of Puppies (kcal/day)

Body Weight (pounds)	Age in Months				
	2	3	5/6	12	24
2	250	200	125	125	125
5	421	336	252	210	210
11	1048	838	503	419	419
22	1763	1763	846	705	705
33		2390	1434	955	955
44		3004	1778	1185	1185
66			2813	2009	1607
110			4715	2947	2357

Table courtesy Waltham Centre for Pet Nutrition. Used with permission.

Just as with adults, you will do best by continually assessing your feeding program.

A notion still persists that puppies should be roly-poly, and to a certain extent, this is true. When you are doing body condition scoring on puppies, you need to keep in mind that they often have round bellies in place of an abdominal tuck. However, they should not be fat. In fact, studies have indicated that some restriction of caloric intake during growth can significantly increase the dog's life span. On the other hand, even very modest overfeeding can predispose the dog to obesity. So how much you feed your puppy is certainly important.

What you put into those little growing bodies is crucial. An older guide to nutrition for dogs recommends adding raw liver and cottage cheese, boiled egg, or ground chuck to the puppy's food. Protein

levels are certainly going to get a boost from this idea, and who knows what would go on with the calcium/phosphorus balance! The strategy these days is to control the calories and levels of fat and calcium to try to achieve the healthiest

Puppies should be trim but often have round bellies.

101

growth rate rather than the fastest. Protein and calcium requirements are higher than for adults, but they still need to be controlled. *Maximum growth does not equal optimal growth.* The current fad for 100-pound Labradors and 200-pound Rottweilers is bad enough on its own, but trying to reach that weight as quickly as possible can be disastrous for these dogs.

In general, small breeds reach their adult size by six to 12 months of age. Larger breeds take 12 to 24 months. Whether large or small, by maturity the dog has increased its birth weight by 40 to 50 times. The genetic selection involved in creating large and giant breeds has brought with it side effects related to the excessive growth rates often seen in these dogs. Such rapid growth results in abnormal formation of the bones responsible for supporting the weight-bearing cartilage of the joints.

To keep your dog in top condition, continually assess and adjust your dog's diet.

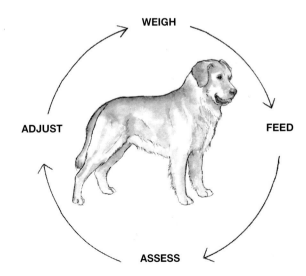

WEIGH

ADJUST

FEED

ASSESS

The newer diets specifically for large breed puppies (dogs that will weigh more than 55 or 65 pounds at maturity—there is not full agreement on the amount) aim to slow down development. Slowing the puppy's rate of growth will *not* result in a smaller adult dog—the dog will simply take longer to achieve full size. "Because of their exceptional growth rates, large-breed puppies are much more susceptible than other breeds to developing a variety of bone and skeletal problems," notes Claudia Kirk, DVM, research scientist at Hill's Science and Technology Center. Excess calcium in the diet (whether in the food or added via supplements) can actually impede the cycle of breakdown and remodel necessary for strong, dense bones. It creates large but weak structures more subject to bone and joint disorders and fractures.

Studies at Washington State University showed a direct relation between poor diet management and skeletal problems. Overnutrition was linked to *hypertrophic osteodystrophy* and *osteochondrosis*, both crippling skeletal disorders. Interestingly, an early change to a proper diet can largely correct these maladies even after they have begun to occur.

As this is being written, Hills and Iams are offering puppy foods specifically formulated for large-breed dogs. Iams points out that hip dysplasia is estimated to depend approximately 40 percent on heredity but that environmental influences, certainly nutrition in particular, play a large role in determining how severe the problem becomes. One study showed that young dogs allowed to overconsume calories, calcium, and phosphorus exhibited splayed feet, wobbler syndrome, and skeletal pain, while a group fed 20 percent less suffered only mild hip dysplasia. Another study, with Labrador Retrievers, fed half of the dogs free choice and the other half in limited portions. The free-choice group of 24 had 16 dogs with hip dysplasia, while the restricted group had only five. Too much calcium undoubtedly causes skeletal malformation, *not* optimum growth.

For all puppies, not just large breeds, nutritionists now recommend portion-controlled feeding. A dog food manufacturer points out that most growth foods are extremely palatable in order to help train young puppies to eat solid food. Therefore, many dogs will overeat.

Use package guidelines as a starting amount of food for your puppy. The important point is to monitor the puppy's condition and adjust rations accordingly. Other than the likely absence of an abdominal tuck, you can use the regular body condition scoring system illustrated in Chapter Ten. Puppies also require vigorous exercise to help develop their young muscles and bones. Sedate walks are not enough—they need to run or swim about a half hour daily. Many will see quite well to their own exercise given the opportunity, tearing around the house or yard like a whirlwind before suddenly flopping down

for another nap. However, being involved in your pup's daily exercise will help ensure you both get some and develop the bond between you.

At three to four weeks of age, puppies should begin the weaning process. Use one part dry food mixed with three parts lukewarm water, or two parts canned mixed with one part water, to make a thick gruel. Offer the food in a shallow, flat pan to make it easier for clumsy puppies to get at. To encourage puppies to try this new substance, dip your finger in it, then let a puppy suck or lick your finger. Provide a fresh batch of food three or four times a day.

As the puppies get accustomed to the food, gradually decrease the amount of water. Continue feeding three or four times a day—feeding puppies free choice, or ad libitum, is not recommended. Monitor puppies' condition to be sure that each is getting enough food. In large, competitive litters fed from one pan, lower-ranked puppies can be pushed away from the food.

At six to eight weeks of age, the puppies should be weaned. Now they can begin to be fed in individual bowls. Each pup should have a measured portion of food in each of three or four daily feedings. Dr. Kirk believes that portion feeding is the healthiest option, because timed feedings (putting down a bowl of food and picking it up in ten or 15 minutes) teach puppies to bolt their food as quickly as possible before it is taken away.

ing dry food, but their self-regulation tends to be a little stronger with dry foods.) Dry foods also contribute somewhat to better tooth and gum maintenance, though not as much as you may think because dogs mainly gulp their food without chewing. Hills makes a dry food specially formulated and sized to clean teeth as a dog eats it.

Feeding the proper amount of a good-quality food throughout adulthood contributes to good health, ideal body weight, and longevity. Keeping your dog lean through adulthood and providing the correct balance of nutrients can increase life span by 10 percent. Realize that adult foods can vary from 300 to over 500 kilocalories of metabolizable energy per cup of food, so the amount fed can vary widely from food to food. Notice that although an 80-pound dog is four times the size of a 20-pound dog, the larger dog's energy requirements are *not* four times the small dog's. The kilocalories required per pound decreases as the size of the dog increases.

An adult dog, no longer growing, requires energy to meet three needs—thermal regulation, the energy needed to metabolize food, and daily activity. When the energy in the daily ratio equals the energy needs of these three items, the dog is in energy balance and will maintain current weight. Adults suffering disease or recovering from surgery may require special veterinary formulations, discussed in Chapter Eleven.

As puppies age, the number of feedings decreases. Once they have attained skeletal maturity at one year of age, puppies can be gradually switched to an adult food. Though large and giant breeds will continue to grow, it will occur at a decreased rate, mostly via muscle mass and body weight changes.

Maintenance

All foods other than puppy formulas are based on adult, or maintenance, formulations. Though specialty foods are gaining in market share, adult dog foods still make up the bulk of sales for most pet food manufacturers.

Dry foods are favored by both dog owners and nutritionists for maintenance diets. Canned and semimoist foods tend to be more palatable and can encourage overeating and lead to obesity. (Of course, dogs can just as easily become obese by overeat-

Gestation/Lactation

During parts of the reproduction process, the bitch will require fully as much from her food as do her puppies, if not more, although her needs will fluctuate widely throughout this period.

An inadequate diet at any point in the reproductive process can have serious consequences for both mother and her offspring. Deficiencies during pregnancy may result in a dog facing motherhood in less-than-prime condition, an increased chance of severe diarrhea following whelping, or eclampsia. Anemia can occur in both the dam and the puppies. *Fading puppy syndrome*, where pups appear normal at birth but have problems within several hours or days or are rejected by the mother, is blamed partly on inadequate nutrition during gestation. Improper nutrition can mean that after whelping, the dam may fail to produce milk completely, or produce less than expected, and the milk may be lacking in nutrients.

The dam's first milk, called *colostrum*, is vitally important to the puppies. It confers temporary immunity while the pups' own immune systems are developing and is available only for the first 24 to 72 hours.

The changes in nutrient requirements occur as the pregnancy advances. Most of the weight gain of the developing puppies occurs in the final third of the gestation period. For the first five weeks of gestation, the bitch will do fine on

usual amounts of her regular food. However, if you plan to change foods for the process of reproduction, you will need to introduce the new food gradually, and this is a good time to accomplish that.

One dog food manufacturer recommends that at the fifth week of pregnancy and each week thereafter, you increase the bitch's rations by 15 percent. By the time whelping occurs, she will be eating 60 percent more than her normal amount. You will likely need to provide the food in several small meals throughout the day, as the bitch's swelling abdomen makes eating a large meal uncomfortable or downright impossible. The food should contain at least 1,600 kcal of ME per pound (724 kcal/kg)

A healthy adult should be trim and energetic.

Once whelping has occurred, the bitch will need even more food to provide milk for all those hungry puppies.

and at least 21 percent protein (these measurements may be on the label or you may have to call the manufacturer and ask for them). Feeding the bitch a puppy food during this period will satisfy her nutritional needs and make weaning easier, as the puppies will be used to the taste of the food through their mother's milk.

However, overfeeding is not advisable. It can lead to very large fetuses and serious problems in whelping. The bitch should gain only 15 to 25 percent of her weight during pregnancy.

Many bitches will refuse food about 12 to 24 hours before whelping. They should begin eating again within 24 hours after the event. After whelping, the bitch should weigh about 5 to 10 percent more than her normal maintenance weight.

Lactation—providing milk for her puppies—is even more demanding for the bitch, and the demand increases as the puppies grow. For the first week, feed one and one-half times the maintenance amount. During the second week, feed twice the amount; during the third week, three times; and by the fourth week, feed four times the maintenance amount. Another guideline is to increase food by 100 kcal of ME per pound of puppies in the litter each day during lactation. Water is exceptionally crucial during lactation, because it provides the main constituent of milk.

To understand the nutrition demands placed on the bitch during this period, consider this: A Labrador bitch with six four-week-old puppies will need to supply each puppy with 500 kcal of energy through her milk, for a total of 3,000 kcal going to the puppies. Milk production is not 100 percent efficient, so the bitch will require about 4,030 kcal to produce the milk. Add the 1,530 kcal she needs for her own maintenance, and you have a whopping 5,560 kcal of energy required each day! Obviously a nutrient-dense, highly digestible food is a must. Through this demanding period, the bitch should not lose more than 10 percent of her normal body weight.

By three or four weeks of age, the puppies begin showing interest in solid food. At this time, the dam should be fed apart from her puppies to be sure that she gets the nutrition she needs and in case she resents the pups wading in her food.

After four weeks of age, the puppies can no longer gain all their nourishment from their mother's milk and should be eating moistened food from pans as well as nursing. At seven or eight weeks of age, they are weaned. They must be separated from the bitch to keep them from nursing. To help dry up her milk, on the day of weaning, the bitch should be fasted. On the following day, she should be fed one-quarter her normal maintenance ration. On the next day, increase to half normal ration, then three-quarters the next day, and finally back to a normal maintenance ration on the fourth day following weaning.

One final note about calcium—while the bitch does require higher levels of calcium during pregnancy and lactation, she fills those needs by eating more food. Supplementation is not required and could cause physical deformities in the fetuses. Supplementation will not prevent eclampsia. In fact, supplementation can actually interfere with cartilage and bone maturation in the puppies and impair absorption of zinc and magnesium in the bitch and puppies. Supplementation disturbs the normal regulation of blood calcium levels by the circulating hormones *calcitonin* and *parathyroid hormone*.

Performance/ Working

Hard-working dogs, unless fed correctly, can suffer a critical lowering of blood sugar. The dog may appear dazed, start to stagger, even suffer seizures. However, dogs

should never be fed heavy meals before strenuous activity. What can you do?

Both the nutrient content of the food and the timing of feedings are critical. The best feeding plan is a small meal before work and snacks throughout the day. The main meal is given only after the dog has had a chance to cool down. Small drinks of water at frequent intervals are also essential.

As for what the food should be, one dog food manufacturer proposes the following guidelines:

This diet is much higher in protein and fat than the average premium or super-premium food. Dogs working for long periods mainly use fat as fuel. Their muscles generate energy through fatty acid oxidation.

Feeding a high-fat diet during

Afghan Hounds are an excellent example of dogs that perform best when an activity calls for short, intense bursts of energy.

Ideal Diet for Hard Work and Stress

Energy Proportions	% of Calories
Protein	32
Fat	51
Carbohydrate	17

Dry Matter Basis	% of Calories
Protein	42
Fat	30
Carbohydrate	22
Fiber	2
Ash	4

Digestibility%	90
Main Ingredients	Meat, meat by-products, grain

Table courtesy of the Waltham Centre for Pet Nutrition. Used with permission.

training (not just actual competition) accustoms the dog's muscles to burning fat more efficiently.

In dogs that work for short bursts, such as participants in flyball or lure coursing, a higher carbohydrate diet probably will work well to fuel the fast contraction of muscle fiber.

What about other nutrients? Well, exercise means increased protein synthesis and protein catabolism, so an increase in protein seems to be in order. A study compared the response to diets of 16, 24, 32, and 40 percent protein in sled dogs in training. The dogs fed the highest protein diet showed a better ability to oxygenate tissues. All of the dogs on the 16 percent diet sustained at least one injury serious enough to keep them from training for a week or more. Two such injuries occurred in the group fed 24 percent protein, none in the two higher protein groups.

Protein is not a good muscle fuel, however. The diet must include sufficient fats and carbohydrates for energy needs, allowing the protein to be used for tissue protein synthesis.

The role of carbohydrates during training and working appears limited, although *after* exercise, carbohydrates can help in recovery. A supplement of 1.5 grams of carbohydrate per kilogram of body weight fed immediately after cool down following exercise greatly improved muscle *glycogen* (a starchlike substance available to be changed into sugar as the body needs it) replenishment in the first four hours of rest.

The type of fiber appears important. One dog food manufacturer maintains that moderately soluble, moderately fermentable fiber sources, such as beet pulp or rice bran, promote production of short-chain fatty acids (SCFAs) in the gut. These SCFAs provide nutrition to the cells of the gut, promote sodium and water absorption, and maximize nutrient absorption and utilization. These fibers were shown to help prevent exercise-induced gastrointestinal disorders such as stress diarrhea.

Beyond this, speculation exists but little research. Another dog food manufacturer postulates that higher levels of iron may be necessary for hemoglobin production and oxygen transport. They also point out that most performance diets are high in meat and thus automatically high in iron.

The final consideration is water. High-calorie diets result in a high *solute* load, meaning increased urinary water loss. High respiratory rates during exercise also increase water loss. So water intake must also be high.

Successful high-performance feeding requires dense energy content, protein balanced with metabolizable energy, balanced fatty acids, and correct fiber. It must be highly palatable, to encourage eating during the stress of the performance.

Senior/Geriatrics

Perhaps more than any other life stage, old age is very much an individual thing. A dog food manufacturer offers the generality that dogs are considered geriatric once they have reached the final quarter of their life span and provides these averages:

Small dog	12 years
Medium dog	10 years
Large dog	9 years
Giant dog	7 years

Just as with humans, though, some dogs seem to maintain their puppy vitality through their whole lives while others slow down when barely middle aged. You need to know your own dog and recognize changes.

Researchers attempting to investigate the needs of older dogs have the problem of discriminating between the effects of aging itself and the effects of diseases occurring

Water is the most essential nutrient and should be offered frequently.

condition as he or she approaches and enters old age.

Controversy about protein for older dogs has raged for years. In many senior diets, it was lowered, but some studies have actually suggested that older dogs have higher protein requirements. Yet high levels of protein may be detrimental if renal function is failing, a common problem of older dogs. What *is* the answer?

Protein quality is at least part of the answer. The protein in senior diets should have a high *biological value* and high digestibility to reduce the formation of harmful metabolites. The diet must provide sufficient protein for body maintenance to minimize losses of lean body mass.

What about renal failure? It's one of the four leading causes of death in old dogs. The metabolic products of protein are believed to contribute to the physiological abnormalities of renal failure. A dog's kidneys can suffer up to 75 percent loss of function before clinical signs become apparent. So should you feed an older dog as if it has subclinical renal failure in the absence of any signs? Probably not. However, once the disease manifests itself, the quantity and quality of protein (and quantity of phosphorus—more about this in Chapter Eleven) in the diet is very important.

Plenty of healthy older dogs with no signs of kidney or liver disease eat high-protein diets with no ill effects. Dogs recovering from surgery or other illness need protein

The healthy senior dog should have more frequent veterinary check-ups, but doesn't need special food unless a definite problem presents itself.

in older dogs. Cardiovascular disease, kidney dysfunction, and tumors are all more common in older dogs, although not all old dogs suffer these maladies. So far, research has shown little or no difference in the nutritional needs of elderly dogs. Two studies showed no changes in the ability to digest food between one-year-old and 10- to 12-year-old Beagles and between groups of dogs aged two to three, eight to ten, and 16 to 17.

Resting energy requirements and physical activity both decline with age. However, a lessening of taste and smell and increasing dental problems mean an older dog may be eating less. Where it was once thought that dogs tended to gain weight as they aged, studies now show more underweight than overweight senior canines. You need to be especially aware of your dog's

to support recovery. One study showed that diets of 18 percent and 35 percent protein had no effect on renal failure in elderly dogs, but the dogs fed the low-protein diet had a higher mortality rate. More study is certainly needed here.

Lowering phosphorus is less controversial. Lower levels do not appear to have any ill effects and have definite benefits in the event of renal failure, whether diagnosed or not. Protein and phosphorus are generally derived from the same food sources, so they naturally rise and fall together.

Fiber is another area of some controversy. In the past, higher levels were recommended to ease digestion and avoid constipation. Now pet food manufacturers suggest that fiber should be less than 5 percent. Again, quality should be high.

On the subject of fat, researchers report that the requirements for essential fatty acids remain essentially the same.

Information about vitamins and minerals is even sketchier. Older dogs may require increased vitamin A, vitamin E, and the B vitamins because of normal digestive changes seen in aging. One pet food manufacturer suggests that increasing potassium, zinc, magnesium, and selenium may be beneficial because the dog is digesting less and these substances may be neutraceuticals. However, studies at Cornell contradict this, suggesting that older dogs do not have decreased ability to digest nutrients.

Oxidative damage to cells, accumulated over the years, is thought to be a major factor in the aging process. Normal cellular processes produce free radicals. These free radicals gradually break down cell membranes. Some researchers believe that an imbalance in free radicals and the antioxidants that neutralize them is the actual mechanism of all degenerative disease. If this is so (and evidence is still largely lacking), increasing antioxidants could slow down the aging process. Extra vitamin A, C, and E *may* prove beneficial.

Keep in mind that no regulations exist regarding senior diets. The designation is actually meaningless from a legal perspective. If your older canine is not suffering any apparent disease and seems to be doing well on regular adult food, you probably shouldn't change just because a certain birthday has passed.

Both canine and human seniors can benefit from regular exercise.

Points to Remember

- Foods for all-life stages are formulated to meet the needs of puppies and reproducing bitches and are likely to provide excess calories to other dogs.
- Puppies require higher levels of energy to fuel growth, but the fastest growth rate is not the healthiest.
- Large-breed puppy foods slow the growth rate but have no impact on the adult size of the dog.
- Excess calcium in puppy diets contributes to skeletal disorders, weak bones, and fractures.
- Puppies may lack the abdominal tuck of adults but should not be fat.
- Puppies require vigorous exercise to help develop muscles and bones.
- Puppies can start the weaning process at three to four weeks of age and should be fully weaned at six to eight weeks.
- Portion feeding is more healthy than timed feeding.
- Feeding the proper amount of a quality food throughout the dog's life span contributes to good health and longevity.
- Adult dogs require just enough energy for thermal regulation, the metabolism of food, and daily activity.
- Inadequate diet during reproduction can have serious consequences for bitch and puppies.
- From the fifth week of pregnancy through the fourth week of lactation, the bitch's nutritional needs will increase.
- Supplementation with calcium will not prevent eclampsia and may harm the bitch and the puppies.
- For hard-working dogs, both the nutrient content of food and the timing of meals are crucial.
- Performance diets are high in fat and calories.
- The age at which a dog is geriatric varies with size, breed, and individual.
- Overweight is mainly a problem of middle age—underweight is a problem of geriatrics.
- Older dogs do not require reduced protein except in response to some disease processes.
- *Some* evidence supports the beneficial properties of antioxidants for older dogs.
- No legal definition exists of a senior or geriatric diet.

Chapter Ten
The BIG Problem

Even dog food manufacturers, in the business of selling dog food, admit that obesity is a growing problem among dogs. Purdue University conducted a survey of over a million dogs through their Veterinary Medical Data Bank. Less than 2 percent of the dogs were noted as obese by the veterinarians seeing them. Yet separate studies reported that 21 to 30 percent of 9,000 dogs seen by veterinarians *should* be considered obese. Waltham, reporting from their research facility in England, says that one-quarter to one-third of dogs seen by small animal veterinarians in the United Kingdom are overweight.

What exactly is going on here? Char Bebiak, head animal trainer and behaviorist for Purina, points out one problem: "It's difficult for most people to spot the telltale signs of early weight gain in their dogs. In fact, because owners see their dogs every day, they may not notice that a problem exists. Suddenly their once-fit dog is seriously overweight." It *is* hard to see those excess pounds creeping up. Humans have clothing as an early warning—a few more pounds than usual and jeans get

tight in a hurry. Most dogs wear only their own hair coat. They depend on their owners to check for and recognize weight gain.

In dogs up to four years old, extra pounds are a worry for 12 to 20 percent of the population. However, the percentage rises for dogs in their middle years. In older age, the problem lessens somewhat, with many geriatric dogs actually becoming underweight.

Certain breeds are known for their tendencies toward obesity. Most Beagles and Labrador retrievers always seem to be ready to eat and have efficient metabolisms that store calories well. Individual dogs of any breed or any mix of breeds may have similar characteristics. These dogs could gain weight on a daily portion barely sufficient to maintain other individuals their size who have less-thrifty metabolisms.

Waltham has done a very interesting study on how changing lifestyles are affecting our pets. Their research revealed that dogs were *not* getting 60 minutes of exercise a day as previously thought. Decreased human activity levels have been passed

Owners of Miniature Pinschers name obesity as a major problem of their breed.

sity in canines, not wanting to embarrass or offend their human clients.

The new dog training emphasis on positive methods and food rewards is also having an impact. Puppy classes and no-force training (using treats as rewards) are welcome innovations, but veterinarians report seeing a lot of pudgy puppies. Owners need to realize that those treats contain calories and must be considered as part of the overall feeding plan.

Obesity has serious health consequences. These may include breathing impairment or heart disease, impaired liver function, a tendency toward diabetes, and increased stress on bones, ligaments, and tendons that can lead to excessive wear on joint surfaces and degenerative arthritis. Skin problems may occur. Heat stress is more likely, as fat has excellent insulating properties and impairs heat dissipation. Surgery is more difficult because correct anesthesia levels are harder to determine and suturing is trickier. Breeders will be interested to know that obesity has a definite negative impact on reproduction—males have lower libidos and semen quality, and females have smaller litters, increased puppy mortality, and problems with whelping and nursing.

For weight loss, you must reduce the intake of calories below the level used by the dog each day. Research indicates that an ideal weight-loss program will result in a 1 to 2 percent decrease in body weight per week. The dog should be weighed at

along to our dogs. According to veterinarian Jo Wills, head of scientific affairs at the Waltham Centre for Pet Nutrition, "Only 10 percent of men and 20 percent of women are now employed in physically active occupations. As we drive more and walk less, our dogs get less exercise. Modern conveniences such as central heating, which reduces the need to expend energy to stay warm, may be significant in the growing problem of obesity."

Though it is not often spoken of aloud, a strong, established correlation exists between overweight pets and overweight owners. This can make it especially difficult for veterinarians to broach the subject of obe-

least every four weeks to track progress and adjust food intake as necessary. Measuring food and monitoring body condition are critical. In fact, overseeing a canine weight-reduction program will require more changes in *your* behavior than your dog's. First, though, you must recognize a weight problem when you see one.

Recognizing a Weight Problem

The first step, obviously, is to recognize that a dog is overweight. This is more difficult than it may sound. The variety of body shapes among different breeds and the often profuse camouflage of hair present problems. Many dog owners simply don't know what a dog in good body condition should look like.

Purina has developed two programs to help dog owners identify overweight dogs before they become seriously obese. The American Animal Hospital Association backs their National Rib Check Day. Merry Crimi, DVM, president of AAHA, states, "The American Animal Hospital Association is proud to help owners understand the serious health issues relating to overweight dogs through National Rib Check Day. Routine visits to the veterinarian combined with active in-home monitoring of the dog's overall health will go a long way in combating the severity of dog obesity."

Char Bebiak explains, "The most comprehensive check is a combination of hands-on and visual evaluations. Once owners know what to look and feel for, it becomes a relatively quick routine that may add up to years of enhanced health and quality of life for the family dog." The rib check test is a simple, three-step procedure.

First, place both your thumbs on your dog's backbone with your fingers extending down her sides. Run your fingers along the rib cage. If you can't easily feel the bony part of each rib, the dog may need to lose weight.

Second, stand directly over your standing dog and look down at her. You should see a clearly defined waist behind the ribs. If your dog does not have a definite *hourglass* shape, she may need to lose weight.

Third, check your dog's profile. If you don't see a clearly defined tuck up, where the abdomen rises behind the rib cage, the dog may need to lose weight.

Keeping an eye and your hands on your dog will help to identify increasing weight early. The best way to deal with obesity is not to let it happen in the first place.

The body condition scoring system (BCS) builds on the visual and physical exam of the rib check test by rating a dog on a scale of one to nine according to the results of the rib check. See the chart for further visual and written details of how to judge your own dog's condition.

Canine Body Condition

❶ EMACIATED Ribs, lumbar vertebrae, pelvic bones and all bony prominences evident from a distance. No discernible body fat. Obvious loss of muscle mass.

❷ VERY THIN Ribs, lumbar vertebrae and pelvic bones easily visible. No palpable fat. Some evidence of other bony prominence. Minimal loss of muscle mass.

❸ THIN Ribs easily palpated and may be visible with no palpable fat. Tops of lumbar vertebrae visible. Pelvic bones becoming prominent. Obvious waist and abdominal tuck.

❹ UNDERWEIGHT Ribs easily palpable, with minimal fat covering. Waist easily noted, viewed from above. Abdominal tuck evident.

❺ IDEAL Ribs palpable without excess fat covering. Waist observed behind ribs when viewed from above. Abdomen tucked up when viewed from side.

❻ OVERWEIGHT Ribs palpable with slight excess fat covering. Waist is discernable viewed from above but is not prominent. Abdominal tuck apparent.

❼ HEAVY Ribs palpable with difficulty, heavy fat cover. Noticeable fat deposits over lumbar area and base of tail. Waist absent or barely visible. Abdominal tuck may be absent.

❽ OBESE Ribs not palpable under very heavy fat cover, or palpable only with significant pressure. Heavy fat deposits over lumbar area and base of tail. Waist absent. No abdominal tuck. Obvious abdominal distention may be present.

❾ GROSSLY OBESE Massive fat deposits over thorax, spine, and base of tail. Waist and abdominal tuck absent. Fat deposits on neck and limbs. Obvious abdominal distention.

*Adapted with permission from the Ralston Purina Company, St. Louis, Missouri.

Changing How You Feed Your Dog

If you have a dog with a weight problem, ad libitum feeding—free access to food 24 hours a day—is not a good idea. To understand why dogs often overeat when left to their own devices, consider the evolutionary feeding pattern of wild canines. In the wild, it can be feast or famine. Food is available only when a kill is made. So wild canines eat as much as they can hold when food is available, never knowing when a good meal may next be available again. This habit has been passed down to our domestic dogs (some more than others, obviously). Dogs are also social animals and tend to eat more in the presence of their pack (other household dogs and/or their human family).

Portion feeding allows you to control the amount of food available to your dog. To help your dog adjust to this new feeding regime, select feeding times that you can repeat each day. Dogs value routine. Dividing each day's allotment into at least two meals will lessen the dog's hunger pangs and will also help to keep her metabolism ticking over at a higher rate.

Next, examine *what* you're feeding your dog. This includes not just that complete and balanced dog food but everything that your dog consumes. Treats contain calories, often *a lot* of calories. A dog that gets into the garbage or goes next door to beg for handouts from the neighbor increases the caloric intake. One kindhearted family member that gives in to the dog's begging can sabotage a weight-loss program. Keep a log of any food given to the dog on a daily basis. Be sure to include all meals, treats, and snacks and to account for all the potential food givers in your household. If other pets live in the house, be aware of possible food theft. Dogs often consider cat food a desirable taste treat, and some canines may go so far as to raid predigested "goodies" from the litter box.

People have a hard time putting their dogs on a weight-loss program. They equate giving treats with giving love. It's hard to withstand those big brown (or blue) pleading eyes. If changing your dog's feeding regime makes you feel like a villain, this might be a good time to work on your own weight loss or healthier eating regimen. Make a deal with your dog that you're in this thing together. You *are* both going to be getting more exercise, after all. Suffering along with the dog won't make any difference to the dog, but it may help assuage your guilt.

Give your time and attention as rewards in place of treats. If you can't bear to cut out treats or are using treats in your training program, at least use low-calorie choices. Table scraps or other people food are often calorie laden.

If you also have cats, place their food bowls up high where the dog can't reach them.

(With slightly overweight dogs, just cutting out table scraps may be enough to resolve the problem.) The best strategy is to use part of the dog's daily food allotment. If you feed your dog dry kibble, you can simply take some pieces from his measured serving to use as rewards throughout the day. If you feed a canned meatloaf type product, you can slice it thin and slow-bake it in the oven until it is dry, then crumble it for treats.

Be as careful about the ingredients of treats as you are about ingredients in the dog's regular food. Don't use vitamins as treats—you risk oversupplementing your dog. Watch out for high levels of sodium. Keep in mind that for a dog consuming 1,000 calories a day, a chunk of cheese containing 100 calories takes up one-tenth of the dog's entire ration.

Feeding recommendations on dog food packaging are nothing more than guidelines for the mythical average dog. The following table gives some idea of how your feeding habits will have to change if your dog is to lose weight.

Waltham uses the equation $E = aW_b$ to calculate energy requirements for the adult dog. W is the dog's body weight. W_b is the metabolic version of body weight, with

Feeding Guide

Current Body Weight	For Weight Loss kcal/day	Cups/day	For Maintenance kcal/day	Cups/day
5 lbs	194	3/4	247	7/8
10 lbs	305	1 1/8	408	1 1/2
20 lbs	484	1 3/4	692	2 1/2
30 lbs	625	2 1/4	935	3 3/8
40 lbs	748	2 3/4	1163	4 1/4
50 lbs	855	3 1/8	1373	5
60 lbs	954	3 1/2	1576	5 3/4
80 lbs	1128	4 1/8	1957	7 1/8
100 lbs	1274	4 5/8	2311	8 3/8

From *Purina Clinical Nutrition Management Veterinary Product Guide.* Used with permission.

the value of b placed (through research) at 0.75. The value of a is the most important and most variable. Dog food manufacturers have generally placed this variable at 125. However, Waltham conducted a study of Border Collies, some kept as pets and some as working dogs. When all the Border Collies were considered together, the a value of 125 was exactly right for a maintenance amount of food, but when the two groups were separated, the pet Border Collies were found to require an a value of only 95. The usual feeding guidelines based on the usual 125 a value would provide far more calories than these dogs needed.

As a result of this study, Waltham has revised the feeding guidelines for all of their dog foods. They still have to hedge to account for variations among individuals, so they are now using an a value of 110 to calculate recommendations. *All* dog food manufacturers remind us that feeding recommendations are only guidelines and that we, the dog owners, are responsible for adjusting amounts to suit our dogs.

One factor contributing to the growing incidence of canine obesity is the burgeoning popularity of premium and super-premium dog foods. These are fine foods, but they are calorie dense. Feeding your dog the same amount of a super-premium food as an average food will likely result in weight gain.

If you have a dog with a weight problem, you may be considering a

Designations such as low calorie or light are more strictly regulated than they once were, and these foods may be helpful in a canine weight loss program.

switch to one of the light foods. The designation light has not been very tightly regulated in the past. New AAFCO regulations for foods labeled light, low calorie, or lean were implemented in January of 1998.

Where, before, products to be labeled lite or low calorie simply had to have fewer calories than another product used for comparison, now AAFCO has set definite maximums. For dry foods, the maximum is 3,100 kcal ME/kg, for semi-moist food it's 2,500 kcal ME/kg,

Hungry dogs may look for calories in the garbage can.

Coat condition is highly dependent on digestible proteins and fats.

rather than calories. These new more stringent regulations give some real meaning to the labels light, low calorie, and lean.

Most manufacturers and nutritionists recommend a low-fat, high-fiber food for weight loss. The theory is that less fat means fewer calories and more fiber means added bulk. Is this true?

Low Fat, High Fiber

Low fat does contribute to lower calories since fat is the most calorie dense of the nutrients in dog food. Simply switching to one of the many light foods may seem like the best solution for your overweight dog. But just one second—you didn't really think it was going to be that easy, did you?

Feeding a low-fat diet involves quite a few implications. Dogs require a certain level of fat in their diet to provide essential fatty acids, carry the fat-soluble vitamins (A, D, E, and K) through the body, and make the food palatable. AAFCO guidelines state a minimum of 5 percent fat for a complete and balanced dog food. Some reports show that feeding low-fat, high-fiber foods can result in dull, dry hair, an indication that the dog isn't getting sufficient fatty acids. This may actually relate more to high fiber than to low fat, and we will discuss it further in a moment. Even sketchier reports link low-fat diets to minor seizure problems. Epilepsy in humans is sometimes treated with a high-fat (ketogenic) diet, so making this connection

and for canned food the maximum is 900 kcal ME/kg. The calorie content must be stated on the label, and feeding guidelines must reflect a reduction in caloric intake.

The designations less or reduced calorie can still be used if the product contains fewer calories than a comparison product. However, the reduction in calories and the comparison product must be clearly stated on the label.

Similar regulations exist for fat content. A product labeled lean or lowfat can have no more than 9 percent (dry food), 7 percent (semi-moist food), or 4 percent (canned food) crude fat. The designations less fat or reduced fat are similar to the labels less or reduced calories, but are applied to fat percentage

seems intuitively correct. However, far more research is required.

The high-fiber portion of a reducing diet has always been added in accord with the theory that increasing bulk will result in a full feeling with less food. The indigestible fiber is supposed to fill the stomach and signal satiety, then pass through the system without converting to calories. Is this really so?

Recent studies conducted at the Waltham Centre for Pet Nutrition would indicate that it is not. They used videotape to record the number of visits to and time spent at the food bowl by their overweight test dogs. It's difficult to quantify "hunger" in a dog. But their study did not reveal any significant changes related to adding a variety of fibers to the test diet. They did note that too high an intake could result in flatulence, poor stool quality, and loss of coat condition.

Let's return to that loss of coat condition. Increased indigestible fiber means that the food passes through the dog's digestive system more quickly. So though the diet may contain sufficient fatty acids, the dog has less opportunity to digest and use them, as well as the other nutrients in the food. The dog may actually become deficient in fatty acids, resulting in a dull, dry hair coat. High-fiber diets may also reduce absorption of zinc, a nutrient necessary for healthy skin and hair. So loading up a dog food with items such as peanut hulls may not be such a good idea after all.

Exercise

The hard-but-true fact is that just as humans, overweight dogs need to exercise. Simply restricting caloric intake will force the metabolism to become more efficient, requiring even fewer calories to maintain body weight. It's sad but true—effective weight loss in either dogs or humans requires expending energy.

Just as with humans, dogs should receive a clean bill of health before beginning an exercise program. With a truly obese dog, veterinary guidelines for how much exercise to provide must be followed closely. Checkups will be necessary as the program progresses to adjust exercise levels. At the beginning, the dog will become fatigued after very moderate exertion, but if you stick with the program her stamina will increase and so should the level of exercise. Do *not* just take your overweight dog out for a five-mile run suddenly one morning. Dogs will often give their all to try to please their humans, to the detriment of their own well-being.

Changing your dog's weight will likely mean changes in your own behavior. "Most dogs left out in the yard by themselves don't get much exercise," says David Dzanis, DVM, veterinary nutritionist at the FDA's Center for Veterinary Medicine. "Owners have to schedule daily exercise with their dogs." James Sokolowski, DVM, Ph.D., professional services manager for Waltham

Outdoor Activities

Activity	Recommended For	Not Suitable For
Walking	Any dog given veterinarian permission to exercise	Dogs with serious health problems
Jogging	Breeds known for good stamina, such as Border Collies, Springer Spaniels, all the retrievers, Brittanys, and Jack Russell Terriers	Heavyset breeds not known for their stamina, such as Newfoundlands, Saint Bernards, Clumber Spaniels, and Bloodhounds
Running	Streamlined, energetic dogs, including any of the sighthounds (Greyhounds, Afghan Hounds, and Salukis), Doberman Pinschers, Brittanys, and Weimaraners	Heavier dogs not known for their distance abilities, such as Rottweilers or Mastiffs, and toy companion breeds not developed for such strenuous exercise (Pugs, Pomeranians, Maltese, and Lhasa Apsos)
In-line skating bicycling	Any of the streamlined, energetic breeds, as above, that can also be relied on not to show aggression toward people or other dogs, because you have less control and could be pulled over by a lunging dog	Heavy-bodied dogs, toy dogs, short-legged dogs, and any dog with aggressive tendencies
Swimming	Any of the sporting breeds (retrievers, spaniels, setters, and water dogs), many of the working breeds (Newfoundlands German Shepherd Dogs, Belgian Tervurens), and Poodles	Dogs whose body type does not lend itself to swimming, especially Bulldogs and Chinese Shar-Peis
Ball throwing/ frisbee tossing/ retrieving	The retrievers, of course, are naturals, but many terriers, Beagles, Cocker Spaniels, and agile mixed breeds are also good candidates	Dogs that just aren't meant to leap, such as Great Pyrenees and Irish Wolfhounds and long-backed breeds that could injure themselves

USA, seconds that by saying, "Pet owners should think about altering their lifestyles to include more activity. A pet's mental and physical well-being are greatest when they are active and maintain a healthy weight." Remember that exercise also has the benefit of speeding up the rate of metabolism even between periods of actual exercise.

So you are about to embark on an exercise program. Do not look at this prospect with dread. This is time you will be spending with your dog, and presumably you *like* being in the company of dogs or you wouldn't own one (or more).

All professionals stress moderation. "After your veterinarian gives you the go-ahead, start your dog on suitable exercise for beginners, such as walking or swimming," advises Merry Crimi, DVM, president of the American Animal Hospital Association. "Begin with a moderate pace and gradually increase the speed and duration of the workout. This is especially important if your dog is older and carrying extra weight. It's also a good policy for owners." Keep in mind that obese dogs have little tolerance for heat and humidity and may fatigue easily. Be alert for panting, shortness of breath, stopping, or slowing down.

Recommendations are for 15-minute walks twice a day, 20-minute walks three times a week, or 20 minutes of exercise each day. Finding a routine you can keep is more important than exactly complying with any of these guidelines. To further motivate you, consider these benefits of exercise:

- Exercise increases blood flow to the muscles and the brain, resulting in a calmer, more content animal.
- Exercise can increase longevity.
- Exercise reduces stress, especially for breeds genetically disposed to high levels of activity

(dogs developed to herd, hunt, or pull wagons or sleds).
- Exercise strengthens the immune system and slows the aging process.
- Exercise improves sleep.
- Exercise uses calories and raises the metabolism.

Exercise also increases energy and stamina, so more exercise gradually becomes necessary.

So you're convinced. What do you need to get started? First, there's that veterinary checkup. (If you have also been sedentary and not a regular visitor to a physician, you should also schedule a checkup for yourself.) Once you both have the medical go-ahead, keep a few basics in mind for the safety of you and your dog.

Walking is a good starting exercise for dogs and humans.

Agility is a high-energy and fun activity.

If your dog is small enough, weigh yourself alone and yourself while holding the dog. The difference is your dog's weight.

- Keep your dog on leash so you can control her pace and position.
- Choose soft paths if possible for the comfort of your dog's feet; if this isn't an option, select roads with the least traffic.
- Walk toward traffic with your dog on your left, away from the road.
- Avoid exercising during hot, humid weather. Plan your activities for early morning or late evening in hot summer months, or go indoors.
- If you will be exercising early or late, be sure you and your dog are visible to traffic. Wear light-colored clothing, and use a reflective collar and leash.
- Carry water for you and your dog, and offer it frequently.
- Keep your goals and capabilities in mind; this is not a speed trial or endurance test.
- Talk to and encourage your dog while you work out.
- Do not exercise until two hours after feeding your dog, and do not feed until at least a half hour after exercising.
- Try to choose an activity your dog likes (see the chart on page 122 for suggestions).
- Do not let your dog annoy or impede other pedestrians.

You will probably have to wait several weeks to see results. Keep on track and motivated. Gradually quicken your pace and increase the duration of your exercise sessions. If your schedule permits, you can also include more workouts per week. Log your progress so you can look back on your achievements.

Indoor Games

Pup push-ups	To practice a little obedience, and excellent as a warm-up or cool-down exercise, have your dog alternate *sit* and *down* in quick succession, or even throw in some *stands*
Fetch	If your dog is a natural retriever or you have done some training, you can get a lot of activity in a small space with just a soft ball and your arm; if your home includes carpeted stairs, you can burn even more canine calories by throwing the ball up the stairs and sending your dog for it (uncarpeted stairs are too dangerous)
Find it/ hide-and-seek	Use your dog's nose to provide exercise by hiding her favorite toys and having her find them; you can also teach a dog to find family members, by name, for an actual game of hide-and-seek
Trick training	Teach your dog something new to add to her repertoire and get in some exercise and lots of quality time; several books and videos are available about teaching tricks (be sure to account for the treats you will be using in your dog's daily food allotment)
Tug games	Behaviorists disagree about the advisability of playing tug games with your dog (some say it encourages aggression); if you are definitely in charge in your home and can play the game on your terms (you say when it starts and stops, and no serious growling allowed), tug games are probably all right and can be a lot of fun and good exercise

Record your dog's weight each week. (If your dog won't stand on a scale at home, either weigh yourself alone and weigh yourself holding the dog and subtract the difference, or, if the dog is too heavy for this, drop by your vet and use the walk-on scale.)

You don't have to give up your exercise regime if bad weather forces you indoors. Use your ingenuity and devise some indoor games (see the chart above).

Once your dog has gained some stamina, your exercise options increase dramatically. Not all forms of exercise are suitable for all sorts

Well-bred, well-conditioned purebreds can win ribbons in the conformation ring.

Benefits and Drawbacks to Dog Sports

Dog Sport	Pros and Cons
Obedience	Useful in many ways in the everyday lives of dogs and attainable by any (though some are naturals and some are not); events are open to *every* dog (mixed breeds are welcome at UKC events) and cover pretty much every skill level all across the country
Conformation	Registered purebreds only; dogs must be excellent physical specimens to do well in this sport, which can provide you with motivation to keep up your exercise program; events occur every weekend in nearly every geographic area
Herding	Dogs from the herding group (Australian Shepherds, Border Collies, Welsh Corgis, and so forth) are, of course, the prime candidates here, but individual breeds from the working (German Shepherd Dogs, Rottweilers, and others) and nonsporting (Keeshond, for example) groups may also show interest in herding; this is very exciting and very good exercise for the dog, but you will need training from someone experienced in the sport—unschooled dogs can be injured by the stock
Tracking	Almost all dogs can be successful at tracking, though some are more enthusiastic than others; this will possibly get you more exercise than your dog, as you will need to lay a lot of practice tracks, but it will get you both out into the open
Agility	A fast-paced, exciting sport open to all dogs in good health; you and your dog will both get plenty of exercise as you practice running courses; a lot of equipment is involved, and you will either need to be an adequate carpenter with considerable storage room or have to join an agility group and use their equipment
Field trials	The specialty of the sporting group (Golden Retrievers, Springer Spaniels, and so forth) plus some of the breeds from the hound group (Beagles, Coonhounds, and others); some events are specifically designed for retrievers, pointers, setters, spaniels, and hounds; to compete seriously, you and your dog will need training from an expert, but you can enjoy the instinct tests/working certificates offered by many of these breed groups without becoming quite so proficient; your dog will get plenty of exercise, but be sure to protect against ticks

Benefits and Drawbacks to Dog Sports (continued)

Dog Sport	Pros and Cons
Lure coursing	A specialty of the sighthounds (Afghan Hounds, Greyhounds, Whippets, and so forth), testing their speed and agility; once conducted using live, wild rabbits as targets (and still sometimes occurring this way), using a plastic lure and sparing the bunnies are now more common; excellent exercise for these built-for-speed dogs, but you will first need some training so you can control your dog during the run and corral her afterward
Flyball/scent hurdles	A relay race over low hurdles, with a tennis ball shot out of a catapult (flyball), or dumbbells scented by each handler (scent hurdles) at the far end; scent hurdles requires training your dog to locate and retrieve only *your* dumbbell
Carting/weight pulling/sledding	Many of the breeds in the working group excel here, though the Siberian Husky and Alaskan Malamute are probably most well known; carting trials involve control, precision, and for the longer road portions, some real stamina; weight pulls involve power, sometimes to an amazing degree
Water tests	A specialty of the Newfoundlands and the Portuguese Water Dogs but open to others; you will have to get wet as part of the training, so summer is obviously the best time to begin this sport; swimming is excellent aerobic exercise, especially good for older dogs or dogs with joint problems
Schutzhund	An intense workout, combining obedience, tracking, and protection work in a single day; you will need lots of training from an expert and plenty of practice; some frown on the sport, saying it encourages aggression, but control is the name of the game here
Earth dog tests/ terrier trials	An event for the terrier group, down to its smallest members; based on the historic use of terriers to control vermin, these tests ask the dogs to go down holes and *worry* their quarry (kept safe in cages); very exciting for these feisty dogs
Canine freestyle	Obedience plus set to music; this is a new sport, modeled after the free-dance competition of ice skating with a dash of gymnastics floor exercise, with the dog as your partner; practicing a routine will give both you and your dog exercise in a much freer atmosphere than the obedience ring
Road trials	Only Dalmatians need apply; once known as coach dogs, this Dalmatian event shows the breed's stamina and flash in running alongside a horse and rider or buggy; though still rare events, these are increasing in popularity

Samoyeds are adept at pulling carts or sleds, but they're also good at packing and can lighten your load on the trail.

of dogs. Make your choice according to your dog's and your abilities and preferences (see the chart on pages 126–127 describing the benefits and drawbacks to various sports).

If you prefer more organized events, you could try your hand (and paws) at some of the various dog sports. It's a great way to have fun, get exercise, meet people who share your interests, and maybe even get competitive.

If you are interested in becoming involved in any of these organized activities, talk to your local training group and/or contact one of the canine registries or sporting organizations listed in this book (see Canine Sports Organizations and Other Useful Contacts, p.168).

Some Final Considerations

You may have heard, at some point, that spayed and neutered dogs become fat and lazy. As with

most such long-heard statements, it contains a grain of truth, but only a grain. Neutered, elderly, or inactive dogs may require 20 to 40 percent fewer calories than their more active brethren. The appropriate number of calories for an individual dog varies according to breed, environmental temperature, life stage, stress level, temperament, even type of haircoat. Dogs become overweight because they consume more calories than they use, not because they are neutered. Possibly the absence of hormones following a spay or neuter can actually lower the dog's metabolism. This simply means less food is required, not that weight gain is inevitable. Dog owners should be advised to watch for any extra pounds creeping on after surgery, not to avoid spaying and neutering.

Some breeds, usually those still closely linked to their native lands, may be metabolically adjusted to their natural diets. For example, Polish Ozwarski Nizinny (PONs) in their homeland of Poland are gen-

erally fed bread, potatoes, cottage cheese, milk, and eggs and get a natural supplement of vitamins and minerals by eating cattle or sheep dung. They seem to be adjusted to this low-protein diet and often gain weight and develop itchy skin when given high-protein premium or super-premium foods.

The advent of the super-premium foods has also played a role in general canine weight problems. These are calorie-dense foods. Dog owners switching to these foods from less-premium varieties but feeding the same amount are almost certainly going to see a weight gain in their dogs. Because of their high fat content, the super-premiums are generally very tasty, and dogs are more willing to consume more than their bodies require. The owner's job is to find the correct amount to feed, using the feeding guidelines as *guidelines*.

Something new on the scene, in response to our constant desire for a quick and easy fix to any problem, is canine diet aids. These over-the-

Food Intake Checklist

Pet's Name _____ Date _____

		Begs Yes	Begs No	Obtains Yes	Obtains No	Type, Amount
Kitchen	Meal preparation	☐	☐	☐	☐	_____
	During mealtime	☐	☐	☐	☐	_____
	After mealtime	☐	☐	☐	☐	_____
Family room/den	While watching TV	☐	☐	☐	☐	_____
	For tricks	☐	☐	☐	☐	_____
Other in-home situations	While children are eating	☐	☐	☐	☐	_____
	After going out	☐	☐	☐	☐	_____
	When you leave	☐	☐	☐	☐	_____
	When you return	☐	☐	☐	☐	_____
Out-of-home situations	From neighbors	☐	☐	☐	☐	_____
	Garbage raiding	☐	☐	☐	☐	_____

Other times not mentioned above:

_____

_____

_____

From additional family members:

_____

_____

_____

From *Dietary Management in Small Animal Practice,* published by Purina. Used with permission.

counter products combine chromium picotinate and hydroxycitric acid (HCA), claiming that these substances impede the conversion of calories to body fat. These claims are untested. It is also important to note that these substances have not been tested for safety in dogs. Preliminary studies have shown an increased risk for liver enlargement and chromosomal damage.

The simple truth is that to slim down, an animal, be it human or canine, must take in fewer calories than it expends. To help you assess your food interactions with your dog and where problems might lie, fill out the food intake checklist.

Points to Remember

- Feeding guidelines on dog foods are based on higher levels of activity than actually occur with the majority of dogs.
- Food training contributes to obese puppies—treats used in training must be accounted for in daily rations.
- Health consequences of obesity include heart disease, diabetic tendencies, impaired liver function, breathing impairment, and increased stress on joints.
- Anesthesia and surgery are complicated by obesity.
- Obesity has a negative effect on reproduction.
- A dog's ribs should be easily palpable, an abdominal tuck should be evident, and an hourglass shape when seen from above should be apparent.
- Super-premium foods are high in calories and must be fed in lesser quantities.
- Lite foods are now regulated more tightly and can help in weight management if the dog will eat them and if their higher levels of fiber do not disrupt the dog's digestion.
- Overweight dogs should receive a checkup before beginning an exercise program.
- Always exercise safely and sanely.
- Neutering and spaying do not cause obesity. They may lower metabolism so that the dog requires less food, but overfeeding causes obesity.

Chapter Eleven
Special Diets, Special Concerns

Not all dog foods are good for all dogs. Some dogs are allergic to one or more of the ingredients commonly used in dog food. Some dog owners are uncomfortable with regular commercial dog foods and want all-natural or vegetarian options. Some dogs, suffering from various medical conditions, require special veterinary diets to ease symptoms or even progression of disease. There is a whole range of foods available to satisfy these wants and needs.

Allergy problems should be carefully assessed before blaming the food. Veterinary diets should be used only on the advice of your veterinarian. They are generally available only through veterinarians, so unless you are using someone else's leftovers, you will have to procure them through a veterinarian anyway. Natural and vegetarian diets are available in regular pet food outlets. Many books and pamphlets include recipes for homemade diets, vegetarian or otherwise. Before you make any choices in this direction, read this chapter.

Food Hypersensitivities

Food hypersensitivity is an area of great disagreement, not likely to be resolved any time soon. At an international symposium on dermatology, Karen Helton Rhodes, DVM, of Cardiopet/Indexx Labs, estimated that 10 to 15 percent of all allergic skin diseases may be traced to adverse reactions to

Fleas are by far the most common cause of scratching and chewing.

foods but added that her own experience showed both food hypersensitivity and contact dermatitis to be quite rare. One study showed certain breeds—Miniature Schnauzers, Golden Retrievers, West Highland White Terriers, Scottish Terriers, and Chinese Sharpeis—to be at higher risk for food allergies. David Dzanis, veterinary nutritionist with the Food and Drug Administration Center for Veterinary Medicine, asserts that the true risk of food allergy is grossly exaggerated, with some 90 percent of skin problems actually caused by fleas.

To deal with such uncertainty requires logic. Everyone agrees that flea allergy dermatitis is the most common allergy affliction suffered by dogs. So if you are the owner of an itchy canine, the logical first step is to eliminate fleas as a possible problem. With the products now available, this is much simpler than it once was. Ask your veterinarian about the excellent *spot-on* products that last up to a month and kill fleas before they bite.

If you eliminate a flea problem and your dog still scratches and chews, start to suspect a dietary deficiency, perhaps a contact or inhalant allergy, or a food allergy. These are difficult to diagnose definitively. It may seem that seasonal symptoms could be easily traced to pollens, just as in human hay fever. However, it's not that simple. Dogs treated to human food items in addition to their canine diet could be allergic to seasonal fruits, summer vegetables, crabs available only at certain times of the year,

133

and so on. Or a dog may have a mild food allergy that causes no problems until it coincides with an equally mild inhalant allergy. Then all of a sudden symptoms appear. Remodeling may be the culprit if your dog has a contact allergy, perhaps to a new carpet. You begin to see how convoluted this problem may be.

So, beyond eliminating flea allergy, how should one proceed? First, it's helpful to understand how food allergies occur.

If a dog demonstrates a bad reaction to a food item the first time it is eaten (say, a young dog given ice cream for the first time), that is a food intolerance, *not* a food allergy. A food allergy takes an average of two years to develop. This completely contradicts the common notion that your dog couldn't possibly have a food allergy because the dog has been eating the same diet for years with no problems. Allergies develop as a result of repeated exposure to the offending ingredient, the allergen.

Once an allergy has developed, daily exposure is quite sufficient to maintain the reaction. Thus, with a food-allergic dog, symptoms will be chronic, not related to feeding time. This lack of a link to feeding time is another common reason people incorrectly eliminate food allergy as a possibility.

Feeding a premium, super-premium, or lamb- and rice-based diet does not guarantee food allergies will not occur. Allergies relate to specific substances, generally proteins, not the quality of those substances. So higher quality is of no help here. No substance is inherently hypoallergenic. A dog stands just as good a chance of developing an allergy to lamb as he does to developing one to beef or chicken. Lamb and rice were once considered a hypoallergenic diet simply because most dogs had never eaten lamb or rice. Now, with so many commercial lamb and rice diets on the market, allergies to lamb are being seen at basically the same rate as allergies to any other protein source.

Food allergies also manifest themselves differently in dogs than they do in humans. Based on their own experiences, pet owners expect upset stomachs or other gastrointestinal troubles. Digestive upsets such as diarrhea do occasionally accompany canine food allergies, but usually food allergies show no apparent link with the gastrointestinal tract. The classic symptoms, instead, are skin problems. Dogs suffering allergies—whether the allergen is flea saliva, pollen, rug fibers, or food—generally have itchy skin. One difference is that dogs with flea problems tend to chew at their stomach or the base of their tail while other allergies concentrate more on the face and feet. However, this does not help much in pinning down the problem. Chronic ear problems may also be present, and the dog may actually break out in hives. Hair loss and sores are usually the result of the dog chewing in a vain attempt to relieve the itch rather than the actual allergy itself.

Food allergies do not respond well to steroids or antihistamines. If your veterinarian puts your dog on corticosteroids and the itching stops, you are probably dealing with an inhalant or contact allergy of some kind. Drug treatment for food allergies may have no effect at all or may lessen the severity, but it won't solve the problem.

Veterinarians agree that neither skin tests nor blood tests have proven useful in diagnosing food allergies in dogs. So what do you do?

"The only reliable test is an elimination diet," says veterinarian Dennis Wilcox. Even here, there is not total agreement on what an elimination diet should consist of and exactly how to use it, but some guidelines are generally accepted.

First, simply changing from one commercial diet to another is rarely effective. Many dog foods use the same ingredients, so changing is of no use in the case of food allergies. Limited-ingredient commercial diets can be effective. However, without veterinary supervision, many pet owners don't try the new food for a long enough period and fail to cut out all extra food sources, such as treats and leftovers. Even such things as chewable heartworm or flea preventatives are suspect, as they contain flavorings and colorings. Under the guidance of a veterinarian, specially formulated foods based on combinations such as potatoes and rabbit or rice and catfish may be acceptable food elimination diets.

Discuss the elimination diet with your veterinarian. Most use a homemade diet. This will be time consuming and probably expensive, so it must be worthwhile. The diet will be based on one protein source that is new to your dog. Lamb used to be used, but with the appearance of so many lamb and rice commercial pet foods, other choices such as venison, rabbit, or fish are often made. To the single protein source you will add a single carbohydrate source. Rice is still used in many instances—rice is rarely found to be the allergen—but potatoes are used if the dog has regularly been consuming rice. The protein and carbohydrate are combined either in equal amounts or with twice as much carbohydrate as protein. This then constitutes the total diet. The dog must not get any treats, chews, table scraps, supplements, chewable medications, or any other food item. Any slip renders the test invalid, and you must start again from the beginning. Some vets go so far as to recommend using bottled water in the dog's drinking bowl.

How long to feed the elimination diet is another area of disagreement. Home-prepared diets are deficient or completely lacking in minerals and certain vitamins. This is indisputable. With immature dogs—and in larger breeds, that can be dogs up to two years old—feeding such a diet for more than three weeks can be harmful. However, you may have to wait up to 12 weeks before seeing significant improvement. Close veterinary supervision is essential, and the elimination diet may have to be supplemented with dicalcium phosphate, safflower oil, and vitamins to provide more balanced nutrition.

The general recommendation is to feed the elimination diet, in the same volume as the dog's regular diet, until at least 50 percent improvement is noted. You may start to see some benefit in two or three weeks or it may take the maximum recommended ten or 12 weeks. A Michigan State University study found that the full ten to 12 weeks was needed in many cases.

Once definite improvement is noted, the dog is returned to his or her original diet in a *challenge*. If symptoms return, usually within two to ten days, the diagnosis of food allergy is confirmed. The elimination diet is used to clear up the symptoms again. You then have two choices.

The preferred option is to continue feeding the elimination diet and add one test item at a time. Each item must be tested for a week to ten days before adding another single test item. Obviously, this process can continue for a long time, but if you do stick with it, you will end up with a list of foods that are safe and another list of foods that are allergens. Yet, after all of this, two years down the road, one

or more of your dog's safe foods may become allergens. Remember that allergies require time to develop.

If you cannot withstand the months of testing individual food items, you can instead test an entire commercial diet, one with as limited a set of ingredients as possible. One study showed that of 13 dogs doing well on a home-cooked lamb- and rice diet, only six continued to do equally well when switched to a commercial lamb and rice-based diet. Randy Wysong, proprietor of one of the more unusual dog food companies, maintains that the problem is the manufactured diet itself, not specific ingredients. He says that a dog with an allergic reaction to a commercial lamb and rice diet will be perfectly able to eat fresh, raw lamb without problems. This is supported at least to some extent by the above finding.

Your testing is likely to show that your dog is allergic to one or more protein sources. A Canadian survey showed that beef and milk comprised 80 percent of the proven allergens, other protein sources were another 5 percent, various cereals represented only 5 percent, and food additives were equally as likely as cereals, adding another 5 percent. A U.S. pet food manufacturer cites beef and soy as the major causes of food allergies, followed by cows' milk, chicken, wheat, corn, and eggs. The same study showed that dogs with food allergies show an allergic response, on average, to 2.4 different allergens. Of the 25 dogs with signs of food allergies used in this survey conducted by the Animal Allergy and Dermatology Clinic in Gaithersburg, Maryland, 64 percent reacted to two or more protein sources.

Food allergies can be eliminated only by removing allergens from the dog's diet. If your testing showed no problems with any of the food ingredients listed in a commercial diet yet the diet causes problems, the allergen may be a preservative, flavoring, fat source, or digest of some sort. This makes your task more difficult.

Dry foods generally contain the highest levels of preservatives because of their large percentages of added fats (which can't be allowed to spoil) and their constant exposure to oxygen (which promotes spoilage). They are also often coated with *digests* to make them more palatable. These digests may be products from poultry, fish, beef, or pork. Dry foods that make gravy when water is added also contain modified cellulose and vegetable gums, usually listed on the label as emulsifying agents and/or thickeners. Canned foods, with their vacuum packing, require the fewest preservatives and with their high palatability, require few or no flavor enhancers.

As you can see, you may have to be a detective to ensure that your dog is getting only substances proven nonallergenic for him or her. Mixed vegetable oils can include oils from any number of sources. Animal fats, meat by-products, and bone meal could be from beef even if the product label claims a single animal protein source such as lamb. Food starch could come from wheat, corn, tapioca, sorghum, or potato.

If you manage to find a diet that works for your dog, cross your fingers and hope for the best: no food or protein is guaranteed hypoallergenic, and your dog may develop new allergies after a couple of years on the new diet. If you can't find a diet your dog will tolerate or if the dog refuses to eat the safe diet (lacking palatability enhancers and digests, it may not be very tasty), you will have to attempt to manage the symptoms of the allergy. Steroids on their own have not proven very successful, but use of steroids or antihistamines in association with polyunsaturated fatty acid (PUFA) supplementation has shown some promise.

If you have an itchy dog, work with your vet to develop a logical course of action for diagnosis and treatment. Do not change dog foods willy-nilly. Diagnosing a food allergy will only be harder if and when it becomes necessary.

Vegetarian and Natural Diets

Vegetarian Diets

People that choose a vegetarian diet for themselves often want to make the same choice for their dogs. They are against the raising of animals for food and/or concerned about the health of food animals. Other dog owners may not be vegetarians themselves but have discovered that their dog suffers from an allergy to meat. Still others feel that while they have no philosophical problem with eating meat, the products used in dog foods are low-quality substances that have been rejected for human use.

To take the last issue first, there may be some problems with meat products used in some dog foods. By-products might be high-quality, perfectly nutritious ingredients or low-quality, filler sorts of substances. It is difficult to tell the difference simply by reading the list of ingredients. You can rely on the reputation of the manufacturer (and the health status of your dog if you have been feeding the food in question) or call the manufacturer and ask for more specific information about those by-products.

Do keep in mind that some meat products are not used much for human consumption simply because no market exists for them. The percentage of people in the United States who regularly consume tongue, brains, or kidneys is pretty low. So organ meats do not command much market space. Nevertheless, they are perfectly edible, very nutritious, and a fine ingredient in dog food formulations. The sole problem is that the antibiotics and growth hormones given to animals raised for food can sometimes concentrate in certain organs.

This should concern everyone, not just dog owners. Humans allergic to penicillin have been known to react to cow's milk if the cows were given high levels of antibiotics and residues were passed along in the milk. Growth hormones and milk-boosting drugs could also cause undiagnosed detrimental effects. This is a problem of the food industry in general, not the pet food industry in particular.

For consumers with meat-allergic dogs or choosing a vegetarian diet for moral reasons, commercially prepared foods are available. Most veterinary nutritionists recommend a commercial diet rather than a home-cooked preparation. (Holistic veterinarians, on the other hand, very often recommend home-prepared dog foods, whether vegetarian or not.)

Nature's Recipe began with a vegetarian formulation. Company president Jeffrey Bennett was not looking to start a dog food company—he was trying to solve the skin problems his Samoyed, Tasha, was suffering. With the help of southern California veterinarian Al Plechner, Tasha was declared allergic to meat, and Bennett began making home-cooked vegetarian meals. Within a month, Tasha's problems had cleared up. However, Bennett did not enjoy his kitchen activities.

"I was cooking vegetarian food for my dog and the daily grind was taking its toll," he says. "I needed a more efficient way to feed my dog healthy meals and I thought there must be other pet owners with similar problems who could benefit from this diet."

In 1981, with money from a second mortgage, Bennett started Nature's Recipe, producing Non-Meat Dog Kibble. The company was also the first to introduce a commercial lamb and rice diet. Now that lamb and rice has become common enough to no longer be a *novel ingredients* diet for many dogs, Nature's Recipe has added other exotic formulations such as venison or rabbit.

The vegetarian product is made from ground whole brown rice, soy flour, barley flour, vegetable oil, carrots, garlic powder, salt, choline chloride, ferrous sulfate, zinc oxide, zinc proteinate, vitamin A supplement, and a variety of other vitamins and minerals. It contains 18 percent protein, 8 percent fat, and 4½ percent fiber, with no artificial colors or flavors, sugars, or dairy products.

This formulation does point up one potential problem of vegetarian diets. Some dogs can't handle the soy products that provide much of the necessary protein in these diets. Though the charge that soy is a cause of bloat has not been substantiated (see the discussion of bloat later in this chapter), soy ferments in the gastrointestinal tract and can result in flatulence, discomfort, and even diarrhea or vomiting. If your dog has difficulties with soy, finding a commercial vegetarian diet may not be possible.

Natural Life produces both canned and dry vegetarian formulas. Soy is further down the list of ingredients in their dry product, so the food may be better tolerated by dogs having problems with soy. The ingredients are ground yellow corn, ground whole brown rice, oatmeal, whole ground wheat, dehulled soybean meal, corn gluten meal, safflower oil, dried kelp, dicalcium phosphate, calcium carbonate, brewer's dried yeast, potassium chloride, garlic powder, yucca schidigera extract, and a variety of vitamins and minerals. Natural Life points out that they use only pesticide-free wheat and whole grains and that their minerals are chelated for easier absorption.

Wysong also offers a vegetarian dry food and notes that it can be fed alone or combined with fresh meat of the owner's choice. (More about Wysong in the next section.) This could be a reassuring option for owners who distrust the meat ingredients in more mainstream commercial diets. Ingredients include corn, soy, corn gluten meal, wheat, oats, brown rice, molasses, tomatoes, flaxseed, alfalfa, dicalcium phosphate, wheat gluten, rice gluten, barley, canola oil, soybean oil, vitamins, minerals, and probiotics (more about these in the next section). The food contains 22 percent protein and 9 percent fat.

Some nutritionists are opposed to vegetarian diets, and even Nature's Recipe warns that they aren't right for every dog. Puppies

Puppies are not good candidates for vegetarian diets. Their protein requirements are too high for such a diet.

the dog will likely need to eat more of a vegetarian food than a meat-based one, so you will need to purchase more, and fecal output will also increase. If the dog seems hungry all the time or loses weight, he is probably not receiving enough nutrition.

Caution is required in choosing a vegetarian food, even more so than with regular, meat-based foods. Some less-than-scrupulous individuals may attempt to appeal to the sensibilities of owners without seriously considering the nutrition of their dogs. An animal welfare organization, the Animal Protection Institute (API), published an expose of a vegan product, Evolution K-9 Premium Quality Pet Food. Though the product declares itself "The world's most complete dog food," the company has done neither feeding trials nor laboratory analysis. Instead, it states on the bag, "Evolution K-9 Premium Quality Dog Food is a balanced ration for all life stages of dogs based on recommendations of the National Research Council." (Remember from Chapter 8 that the NRC has not been involved in the formulation or regulation of dog foods for more than ten years.)

API reported that Evolution's president claimed comprehensive feeding trials were conducted by Al Plechner (who helped start Nature's Recipe), but Dr. Plechner disavowed any knowledge of or association with Evolution. Other claims that the product makes on its packaging

and reproducing bitches, in particular, are poor candidates for vegetarian foods. Formulating a diet high enough in protein to meet the special needs of these dogs is difficult if not downright impossible. Research at Waltham has shown that puppies fed a strictly vegetarian diet did not subsequently accept meat as a food item, which could become a problem if the dog later developed a soy allergy or some other complication.

Only adult, nonreproducing dogs free of health problems should be considered as candidates for a vegetarian diet. Keep in mind that

and marketing materials are equally worrisome: "Only Evolution guarantees five to ten extra healthy years for your pet," is a prime example.

Though enforcement of pet food regulations appears to be a low priority issue, Evolution is being investigated as this is being written. Remember always to look for a statement of AAFCO feeding trials. Rely first on the reputation of the manufacturer and/or recommendations of your veterinarian and after you have fed a food for some time, the health and well-being of your dog.

Natural Diets

Natural diets may be the fastest growing category in the entire pet supplies market. The latest *Pet Supplies Marketing Directory* "State of the Industry Report" notes an 876 percent rise in sales of natural products (including foods along with flea control, treats, supplements, and more) since 1993. Sales reached $65 million in 1996. Thus far, no regulations exist concerning the claim *natural*, but AAFCO is developing standards in response to this burgeoning market segment.

During the mid to late 1970s, the natural foods category began with little fanfare. Early manufacturers of natural diets include Wysong, Regal Pet Foods, and Breeder's Choice. Nature's Recipe broke the category into the big time in the early 1980s. Dog breeders, always on the lookout for a better product in any category, embraced the natural products enthusiastically and passed along recommendations with their puppies. Now, nearly two dozen natural food product lines are on the market. Some pet supply stores have begun to specialize, stocking only natural foods and other products.

Market analysts, watching the growth of natural foods, predict that mainstream foods will be reformulated to include herbs, enzymes, and more antioxidants, and that within ten years, half the pet food market will be natural foods. More whole foods and less processing will be used. Some pet food manufacturers may even branch into the area of supplements. These are not the calcium supplements touted by some but prodigestive substances such as enzymes or probiotics. Many of these substances deteriorate quickly under processing and may be more potent if provided separately from the food. Wysong

You must be dedicated and careful to make a safe and balanced raw-foods diet for your dog.

and Solid Gold both sell supplements along with their foods. In fact, if the predictions are correct, Wysong and Solid Gold will be mainstream in ten years.

Wysong, in business since 1979, is one of the most outspoken critics of the pet food industry. They say the processing involved in the usual manufacture of pet foods robs the foods of much of their nutritional value, and the use of preprocessed ingredients compounds the problem. Wysong promotes and includes whole grains rather than fractions or by-products, organic ingredients wherever possible, whole fresh meats, and special hybrid grains and legumes developed to increase nutrient content (high lysine corn) and to decrease antinutritional factors (low trypsin-inhibitor soybeans).

Despite the fact that Wysong makes dog food, their top recommendation is for a raw-foods diet. They specify raw meats, organs, bones, and fresh vegetables and fruits. They even go so far as to give the percentages that would be consumed in the wild with hunted prey: 62 percent meat, 11 percent organs, 2 percent bones, and 25 percent vegetables. (Though Wysong calls the dog a carnivore, their inclusion of 25 percent vegetables negates the term.) Their next recommendation is to use the same assortment of foods, but cooked rather than raw. Finally, after that, Wysong recommends using their own foods enhanced with their supplements and fresh raw foods. Next, they recommend using their own food, supplements, and cooked food. Feeding their own food alone is nearly at the bottom of the recommendations list, only above feeding other commercial foods alone or giving no food at all!

Wysong tests all their ingredients for mold and mycotoxins. They use something called Oxherphol as a stabilizer. Oxherphol is described as a natural plant extract antioxidant developed by Wysong that combines vitamin E tocopherols and botanical extracts of clover, sage, and rosemary. Wysong both includes and recommends supplementing with probiotics.

To understand what probiotics are and why they are recommended, recall that the intestinal tract hosts a swarming population of bacteria. Some assist in digestion and the synthesis of nutrients, others may be pathogens. Probiotics are cultured organisms and immunoglobins selected to enhance and balance the natural organisms of the digestive tract and inhibit *E. coli* bacteria. The probiotic supplement, called Pet Inoculant, is composed of cold-pressed safflower oil; cold-pressed flaxseed oil; dried whey product; dried fermentation products of *Lactobacillus lactis*, *Lactobacillus acidophilus*, *Bifidobacterium bifidum*, *Streptococcus faecium*, and Oxherphol. If you are familiar with health foods, you have probably run across some of these names before.

Wysong's Maintenance Diet consists of chicken, corn, wheat, brown rice, oats, poultry fats, soy, corn gluten meal, soybean oil, salt, kelp, yeast, lecithin, clove oleoresins, sage oleoresins, rosemary oleoresins, *Aspergillus niger*, *Streptococcus faecium*, *Lactobacillus acidophilus*, vitamins, and minerals. A second maintenance formula is soy free. Wysong also notes that its diets are meant to be alternated with each other to provide variety and optimize nutrition.

Finally, Wysong claims that their processing is specifically designed to maximize nutritional value of the final product, and many of their techniques make good sense. Grains and legumes are stored whole, ground only when actually being processed into the food. Fresh meats and vegetables are injected into the extruder rather than the more usual dried and rendered ingredients. Heat-sensitive ingredients—enzymes, essential fatty acids, probiotics, and vitamins—are added in an enrobing procedure after processing. Products are not warehoused but made fresh to order as much as possible. Wysong foods are packaged in oxygen-free, four-pound packs so that open product is not exposed to oxidation for long.

Bil-Jac promotes their food by asking consumers to check dog food labels for added fat. They say if fat is listed, that fat is the major source of meat protein in the food and is far from natural, being rendered, powdered, and processed. Bil-Jac adds no fats to their foods, instead using frozen or vacuum-processed fresh meat.

Science Diet includes Natural Formula in its product line. They state that the company uses egg protein because lamb meal is too high in mineral content and often contains artificial preservatives. In fact, while many products claim "No artificial preservatives added," Science Diet guarantees that none of the ingredients in their Natural Formula contain any artificial preservatives.

Solid Gold includes lamb meat, ground millet, rice oil, canola oil, flaxseed oil, ground brown rice, ground barley, menhaden fish meal, garlic, catnip, beta-carotene, and a variety of vitamins and minerals, preserved with tocopherols. This product also uses innovative packaging with the same goal as Wysong, avoidance of oxidation. Solid Gold is vacuum packed.

Sissy Harrington, proprietor of Solid Gold, notes that the whole grains used in her company's food mean a substantial amount of indigestible fiber. The fiber is supposed to scrape away debris in the intestines, and it may. However, it also means a larger quantity of stool and that more food must be fed for the dog to ingest sufficient calories. Solid Gold also sells supplements, recommending that their Sea Meal always be given with the food.

Some natural food advocates blame nearly all the health problems of dogs on commercial foods.

Adults and puppies can safely consume natural foods as long as the foods are complete and balanced.

This only makes them appear ridiculous, as genetics has certainly been firmly implicated in many diseases and structural problems. Another purveyor of natural food, PHD, more reasonably quotes references to inbreeding, multiple vaccinations, and allopathic drug treatments such as the indiscriminate use of antibiotics and corticosteroids in addition to "Widespread use of nutritionally deficient commercial pet food."

Nearly everyone can agree that natural products should not contain any chemical preservatives or artificial flavors or colors. However, holistic veterinarians also recommend that products avoid sugar, corn syrup, salt, pesticides, any additives that don't increase nutritional values, any undefined by-products, and hard-to-digest ingredients. They advocate whole grains, fruits, legumes, vegetables, organic meats, and cold-pressed organic oils. Grains, in particular, should be as intact as possible—corn rather than corn gluten and whole brown rice rather than brewer's rice.

Natural food proponents also say foods should be processed as little as possible, as heat destroys or changes a variety of enzymes and nutrients. Because commercial foods must be processed, manufacturers of natural foods add enzymes, vitamins, and minerals from natural sources. These might include blue-green foods (such as barley, algae, and wheat grass), chelated or esterized vitamins, garlic, lecithin, or vegetable oils such as olive or sunflower oil. As an alternative, some manufacturers may offer a line of supplements to use with their diets.

If you desire a natural food, consult the list of ingredients carefully and question the manufacturer about any unclear ingredients or by-products. Look for two or three sources of protein among the first five ingredients. Remember that grains and legumes are protein sources and that whole ingredients are preferred. Consider a manufacturer's reputation—don't just rush to join the latest fad.

Some people mean something completely different when they talk about natural dog foods. Absence of artificial flavors and colors and chemical preservatives isn't enough. They mean a diet based on what the dog's supposed wild ancestors are presumed to eat—raw and unprocessed food.

A raw-foods diet for dogs is an idea that keeps popping up in the occasional book or magazine article. However, is it a *good* idea?

Our dogs are not wolves. Though they may be descended from wolves (and even that is not proven), they have been domesticated for a long time. We have molded dogs into forms as varied as Chihuahuas and Scottish Deerhounds, Basset Hounds and Afghan Hounds. Some breeds could not fit their mouth around a decent bone even if presented with one. Stray populations around the world have shown that if allowed to breed at random, dogs revert back to a definite type: about 35 to 40 pounds, brown, fairly short hair, rangy and lean, with a pointed snout. This is a far cry from a Pekingese.

In the wild, wolves breed according to dominance, effectively meaning that the biggest, smartest, most likely to survive male is the one passing his genetic makeup to offspring. Female wolves certainly do not select mates based on coat color or length, ear set, number of dewclaws, length of muzzle, or any of the other hundred delineations written into the standards of purebred dogs.

Wolf pups are raised on a raw-meat diet from the time they begin life in their mother's womb. They encounter the many disease organisms present in such a diet from their earliest moments and either succumb to them at a young age or build resistance to them. Switching

Our dogs are definitely not wolves.

a dog to a raw-foods diet often means that the dog will be dealing with such detrimental organisms for the first time, often with severe digestive problems. Incautious owners will also be exposing themselves to the organisms by handling the raw meats.

Few among us have the time and patience to handle raw meats safely and blend a complete and balanced food for our dogs. We may want to be involved in feeding our canine friends, but this is simply more than most of us can handle. The on-line site of one veterinarian promoting a raw-foods diet makes it sound extremely simple, even going so far as to say that no specific mixture is required.

This website recommends a diet of one-third or slightly more raw meat (beef, chicken, turkey, or lamb, including organ meats), with the remainder of the diet being raw, grated vegetables such as carrots, broccoli, beets, or any leafy greens and cooked grains such as brown rice, oatmeal, couscous, or any whole-grain cereal or bread. It recommends olive oil, sesame oil, or butter but gives no amounts. Any processed or cultured dairy product, such as cottage cheese, yogurt, or raw goat's or sheep's milk is advised, as well as one to several raw eggs twice weekly, with the shells broken into small pieces. After two or three weeks of this diet, supplements are to be added. These include colloidal minerals, a canine multivitamin mineral supplement, calcium from bonemeal or calcium tablets or powder, to be given at one to two times the recommended dose (in order to compensate for inefficient absorption, the website says), plus vitamins C and E, antioxidants, and marrow bones.

More mainline veterinary nutritionists insist that following a proven recipe exactly is imperative. Do not concoct your own formulation and risk your dog's health. Discuss a recipe with a veterinary nutritionist (not all veterinarians are well versed in the fine points of canine nutrition; in fact, schooling for future veterinarians does not necessarily include *any* courses in nutrition) to be sure the recipe is complete and balanced. Then follow it precisely every time without fail. You cannot just leave something out, no matter how insignificant it may seem, or make do with some other ingredient you think is similar. You must follow FDA guidelines for safe handling of raw meats.

Though 90 percent of the attendees at a conference of the American Holistic Veterinary Medical Association professed to recommend a raw-foods diet, they were also quick to advise that if you don't have the time and discipline to follow a pretested, balanced recipe safely, you're better off buying a natural commercial diet (presumably meaning a formulation high in meat, without artificial flavorings, colors, or preservatives).

For those of you interested in trying a raw-foods diet for your dog, several books are devoted entirely to this subject. Use caution and common sense. Introduce the diet to your dog slowly to give his digestive tract time to adjust and his immune system time to deal with any detrimental organisms. Be sure to handle raw meats safely. As always, the condition of your dog while eating the diet will be your best guide to its suitability. Be particularly alert for any signs of vitamin and mineral deficiencies or toxicities. Remember, these significant dietary components interact in tightly tangled fashion.

Veterinary Diets

Veterinary diets are another growth area in canine foods. At one time not many years ago, any disease requiring or benefiting from a special diet meant either home cooking or the Hill's Science Diet clinical nutrition formulations. Now, though, Waltham, Purina, Eukanuba, and Select Care all offer their own range of diets meant for use in response to disease, and others are probably entering the market.

Any animal's immune system relies on good nutrition for top performance, and any hospitalized animal certainly needs a top-notch immune system to fight off bacterial and parasitic infections. Hospitalized patients often have higher protein and energy needs, and few if any medical conditions benefit from starvation. Good nutrition promotes wound healing and increases wound strength, repairs muscle proteins, and replaces red blood cells and antibodies. However, many illnesses result in a reluctance to eat, and some can upset digestive system efficiency.

Specific diseases or conditions may require adjustments in the diet to help the patient feel better or even slow the disease process. Many veterinary diets are low fat by necessity, and palatability can suffer. Having a choice among brands can help in finding a food the dog will eat.

Chronic Renal Failure

Perhaps one of the best-known conditions benefiting from special dietary considerations is chronic renal failure. This condition is seen in

10 percent of the dogs over age 15. Dogs have such a high degree of renal redundancy that they can lose nearly 70 percent of kidney function before any symptoms appear. The first signs are generally increased drinking (*polydipsia*) and increased urination (*polyuria*). This occurs because the impaired kidneys can no longer concentrate the urine. The end products of protein metabolism are not excreted as well. The dog will become dehydrated if not provided with a constant supply of drinking water. The water-soluble vitamins are subject to loss with the increased urination. Excess phosphorus cannot be efficiently excreted, and in an attempt to balance the calcium-to-phosphorus ratio, the dog's body may leach calcium from the skeletal system. Further symptoms can include vomiting

A dog in good condition will be better able to fend off disease and remain a happy, healthy member of the family.

and diarrhea, irregular heartbeat and hypertension, a dull unkempt coat, weakness, and weight loss.

Protein levels in foods do not cause renal failure, but they are crucial in management once renal failure occurs. The difficulties in excreting protein digestive end products mean that protein levels should be kept as low as possible. The calories provided by fats and carbohydrates should be sufficient to spare protein from being used for energy. Protein sources must be highly digestible, with a high biological value.

Hill's k/d is the oldest commercial diet available for dogs in renal failure. It provides reduced levels of phosphorus, protein, and sodium to provide optimum quantities of essential nutrients while decreasing protein waste products and controlling pH levels. Compared with a regular canine diet, a dog eating k/d has to excrete only 15 to 25 percent of the nitrogen waste.

Now Purina offers its NF formula, Select Care has a Modified diet, and Waltham provides both Waltham Low Protein and Waltham Medium Protein Veterinary Diet. All are low in protein, phosphorus, and sodium. Most have higher levels of the water-soluble vitamins. Select Care includes higher potassium and omega-6 and omega-3 fatty acids.

With good dietary management, dogs showing early signs of chronic renal failure can live relatively symptom free for as much as two years.

Liver Disease

The liver is the control center for utilization of nutrients. Proteins, carbohydrates, fats, vitamins, and minerals are all metabolized through the liver, as are many drugs. The liver produces bile and a variety of enzymes and removes toxins from the blood. Obviously, liver problems are going to have a severe impact on the dog's nutritional status.

Liver disease can arise from many sources. Chronic liver failure can result from cirrhosis, long-term drug reactions and copper toxicosis. Viral infections, pesticides, or biological toxins (such as those found in contaminated wheat) can cause inflammatory liver disease. Tumors and a condition known as portosystemic shunt lead to noninflammatory liver disease.

Some liver problems can benefit from the same diet as that used for chronic renal failure. Others require an even lower level of protein and minimal fat, providing most of the calories through carbohydrates. However, the diet must be customized to respond to the specific circumstances. Dogs with liver disease commonly have very poor appetites, so doing everything possible to maintain food intake is certainly beneficial. Food can be warmed to improve palatability and offered in small meals throughout the day. A homemade diet may be necessary.

Congestive Heart Failure

When cardiac output is decreased, the body attempts to compensate as best it can, often resulting in increased blood pressure and retention of fluids and sodium. Dogs with congestive heart failure often also suffer from impaired renal function.

Both congestive heart failure and the drugs used to treat it can cause nausea and anorexia. While the dog is stabilizing, you should avoid feeding what will be the long-term therapeutic diet. Dogs often associate feeling ill with the food they are consuming at the time and will develop an aversion to the food. Wait until medications such as cardiac glycosides and diuretics have had time to ease symptoms before switching to the appropriate veterinary diet.

Owners of dogs with congestive heart failure should be aware that softened water must be avoided. If you use a water softener in your home, you will have to find another source of water for your dog.

Colitis/Large Bowel Disorder

Both large bowel disorder and small bowel diarrhea (discussed next) can be caused by sudden changes in diet, eating too fast, eating too much, or eating garbage or nonfood items. Large bowel disorder may also result from internal parasite infestation, nonspecific inflammation, or fiber-responsive large bowel diarrhea.

Large bowel disorders are differentiated from small bowel disorders by symptoms. Colitis and large bowel disorder are demonstrated by frequent defecation, often with straining. Only small amounts of feces will be passed at one time, generally with mucus and often with blood.

The dietary objective is to reduce irritation of the bowel and slow transit time through the gastrointestinal tract while providing necessary nutrients. Dietary fiber can help with both decreasing irritation and prolonging transit time. It can also decrease the amount of free fecal water in the colon, lessening diarrhea problems. But too much fiber, particularly if it is highly nonfermentable and insoluble, can actually cause problems, increasing stool volume (certainly an unwanted circumstance) and decreasing palatability. Fat content should also be reduced significantly, as animals having problems with colitis generally have trouble digesting fats.

While diet does not cure gastrointestinal problems, it can have a major impact on symptoms. One dog food manufacturer has found that in many cases of *idiopathic* (cause unknown) colitis, a change to a single-source protein diet effectively controlled the problem.

Small Bowel Diarrhea

Diarrhea may be the only sign, but differentiating between small bowel diarrhea and large bowel disorder is important. Additional symptoms of small bowel diarrhea could include vomiting, lethargy, depression, dehydration, weight loss, and sometimes abdominal pain.

Fasting for one or two days is usually recommended to rest the gastrointestinal tract. Then the dog should be switched to a diet low in fat and low in fiber. Mistaking small bowel diarrhea for large bowel disorder and feeding a high-fiber diet could significantly worsen symptoms.

Remember, no matter what the disease, make dietary changes gradually to give the intestinal flora time to adjust. Only if your veterinarian specifies immediate change in an emergency should you simply stop feeding one food and start feeding another.

Diabetes Mellitus

Approximately 1 percent of dogs suffer from diabetes. Nearly all are Type I cases, in which there is a complete loss of insulin secretion due to destruction of beta cells. Insulin must be provided by injection, and meals must be timed so that nutrients are delivered while insulin activity is at a peak. Small meals should be spaced out through

the period of insulin activity to avoid large fluctuations in blood glucose levels.

Common symptoms are *polydipsia* (increased drinking), *polyuria* (increased urination), and weight loss. Many pets suffering diabetes are obese, and weight loss might not be apparent immediately.

Diets should be high in complex carbohydrates. Semimoist foods are not a good choice, as their simple carbohydrates produce a high insulin response. Commercial diets should be fixed formulas so that types of ingredients and quantities of nutrients do not change.

The amount of energy the dog expends is also part of the nutrient/insulin balance. Diabetic dogs do best with regular exercise of similar duration rather than spurts of high activity.

Other Problems

Some hereditary disorders, though relatively rare in dogdom in general, are seen more frequently in specific breeds. Some of these require dietary modifications.

Copper storage disease, or copper toxicosis, is an acknowledged problem in Bedlington Terriers and is also present in Doberman Pinschers, West Highland White Terriers, and Cocker Spaniels. The livers of these dogs have limited ability to dispose of copper, and the metal accumulates as the dog ages. Symptoms usually appear between four and eight years of age. They include vomiting, anorexia, lethargy, abdominal pain, polydipsia, and polyuria. A definitive diagnosis requires a liver biopsy. Once diagnosed, dogs are fed a copper-restricted diet and medications to increase excretion of copper. The School of Veterinary Medicine at Cornell University recommends Waltham Formula Lite dry dog food for dogs diagnosed with copper storage disease.

Hyperlipidemia is a hereditary problem of Miniature Schnauzers. Laboratory tests show high cholesterol and elevated levels of triglycerides. The dogs may have repeated periods of vomiting, diarrhea, abdominal pain, and even seizures, or they could be without apparent symptoms. Dogs with hyperlipidemia are fed a diet with restricted fats and calories. Table scraps and unapproved treats are forbidden.

Dalmatians share a peculiar metabolic quirk with human beings. While most mammals convert nearly all uric acid to *allantoin* and excrete little urate in their urine, humans and Dalmatians share increased levels of urate and decreased allantoin. In the Dalmatian's case, this results from a defective uric acid transport system in the liver and reduced renal reabsorption of urate. In humans, the low aqueous solubility of urate can result in precipitation of urate crystals out of the serum or urine, resulting in the condition known as gout. Dalmatians avoid buildup of urates in their serum by excreting large amounts in their urine, but this predisposes them to urolithiasis. Symptoms include frequent urina-

tion that appears painful, with only small amounts voided at each attempt. For these dogs, a diet is formulated to promote alkalinity in the urine.

Tartar

Plaque, tartar, gingivitis, and other dental problems become common as a dog ages. Owners are reluctant to have their dogs undergo anesthesia just to have their teeth cleaned. Though some owners do now brush their dogs' teeth on a regular basis and some groomers will perform tooth scaling on wide awake (and well-behaved!) dogs, the problem remains large.

Hill's has developed a diet designed to help. Its t/d formulation does not shatter when chewed as the typical dog food does. Instead, the tooth sinks into the food and nearly all the way through before cracking the chunk. The hard food wipes plaque and tartar off the tooth in the process. The chunks are large, as they must engulf the

Brushing a dog's teeth is most effective at removing plaque and tartar.

whole tooth before splitting in order to have the desired effect.

Hill's study comparing t/d with a regular dry food showed that t/d reduces plaque by 19 percent, tartar by 32 percent, and stain accumulation by 44 percent. Even when regular dog foods were complemented with regular toothbrushing, t/d performed better, reducing plaque by 10 percent, staining by 14 percent, and tartar by 15 percent. The downside is that some dogs find the large chunks unacceptable and refuse them or eat only reluctantly.

Another study looked at the efficacy of rawhide as a tooth cleaner. It showed that rawhide was far better than biscuits at removing plaque and tartar. However, the study dogs were given the rawhide or biscuits three times a day! This is not likely to occur in a home situation. The study also demonstrated that rawhide causes digestive upsets in some dogs.

Pedigree undertook a long-term (12-month) study on the effectiveness of its dental hygiene chew, the Dentabone (or Rask in Europe). Both test groups started with complete dental prophylaxis and were then fed the same diet, with the exception of a daily Dentabone for the test group. Throughout the test period, the dogs receiving the Dentabones had lower plaque and calculus accumulation, less gingivitis, and better breath. No dogs ever refused the Dentabones, and because their rations were reduced slightly, the dogs did not gain weight.

Bloat

Bloat, or *gastric dilation-volvulus*, is not a common occurrence, but is so unexpected and has such dire consequences that it is widely discussed. This still not fully understood condition is a genuine emergency. It can take only a few hours for a dog to go from healthy to near death. Fatality rates reported by veterinarians range from 15 to 60 percent.

Bloat is a sudden, rapid accumulation of gas in the stomach. As the stomach swells and pressure increases, it compresses nearby blood vessels and other organs. The stomach, suspended at each end like a hammock, can twist over on itself, sealing off any possible escape of the gas. This is a life-threatening condition, blocking off blood flow and making breathing nearly impossible.

So what causes this horrible condition? The answer isn't clear. Some people have blamed it on soy products used in dog food formulations or on dry dog foods themselves, but neither cause has been proven, or even implicated, in any scientific research. The Morris Animal Foundation is funding a long-term study at Purdue University focusing on bloat, and thus far, findings have not been diet related. Purdue has found that:

- Bloat risk increases with age; dogs seven or older are twice as likely to suffer an episode as dogs aged two to four.
- Purebred dogs are three times as likely to bloat as mixed breeds.

- Higher expected adult weight of a breed means higher risk for bloat.
- A deep, narrow chest as a breed characteristic (such as seen in the Irish Setter) increases the risk of bloat

The six breeds most likely to suffer bloat are Great Dane, Weimaraner, Saint Bernard, Gordon Setter, Irish Setter, and Standard Poodle. They are followed by the Irish Wolfhound, Borzoi, Bloodhound, Mastiff, Akita, and Bullmastiff.

Recognizing bloat early is crucial so that you can seek veterinary assistance in time. If your dog is pacing or seems unable to settle, lying down and getting up repeatedly, pay close attention to his condition. A dog suffering bloat may groan or whine and attempt to vomit, but without results. Some dogs will lie down and refuse to get up. If you look, you will find the stomach swollen and hard. Signs of shock—pale gums, shallow breathing—may be present. Do not hesitate—get to a veterinarian at once.

You can take some precautions to try to avoid an episode of bloat.
- Avoid exercise for one hour before and two hours after feeding.
- Establish a regular feeding schedule, preferably with two meals a day rather than one.
- When changing foods, do so gradually.
- Avoid any conditions that encourage the dog to eat quickly, such as competition with another dog or timed feeding.
- Don't feed and leave—observe your dog after he eats.
- Limit water after eating or after exercising.
- Try to avoid stress, particularly at mealtimes.
- Be alert for any signs of discomfort.
- To slow a dog that gulps food, mix a little canned pumpkin with dry food and plaster it to the bowl.

Some people suspect that a predisposition to bloat may be hereditary, but that has not been proven either. Just be aware if your dog is a breed with a higher incidence of bloat and take all precautions. While it may help to slow the rate at which a dog eats, thereby reducing the gulping of air, *what* the dog eats does not seem to be a factor in bloat.

Like this Saint Bernard, the breeds most susceptible to bloat are of large or giant size.

Points to Remember

- Flea allergy is far more common than contact, inhalant, or food allergies.
- A food allergy takes an average of two years of exposure to the allergen to develop.
- Proteins are the most common food allergen, with beef and soy the two most frequent problems.
- The primary symptom of allergies in canines is itchy skin.
- Food allergies do not generally respond to antihistamines or corticosteroids.
- An elimination diet should consist of one protein source and one carbohydrate source and must be the only substance fed to the dog.
- Elimination trials should be conducted under the supervision of a veterinarian, as many lack essential minerals or vitamins and cannot be fed long-term.
- Commercial vegetarian diets are available for dogs; they may not be appropriate for puppies or lactating bitches because protein content will not be high enough.
- Avoid unproven fad foods; their manufacturers may be trying to make a quick buck without regard for your dog's nutrition.
- Raw-foods diets are being promoted in several books and on the web. These can be healthful if carefully made but are generally time consuming and beyond the scope of most dog owners.
- The term natural has no regulated meaning as applied to pet foods, though AAFCO is discussing guidelines. In general, natural foods have no artificial colors, flavors, or preservatives.
- Veterinary diets should be used only on the advice of your veterinarian. Specific formulations can ameliorate the symptoms of diseases such as diabetes, congestive heart failure, and chronic renal failure.
- Tartar can be controlled by regular brushing. Hill's special t/d dry food can help if accepted by the dog. Pedigree's Dentabone treats can have a significant impact.
- Bloat is an emergency condition in which gas is trapped in the dog's stomach; you must seek veterinary assistance at once.
- No scientific studies have linked any kind of dog food or dog food ingredient to bloat.

FEEDING DECISION TREE

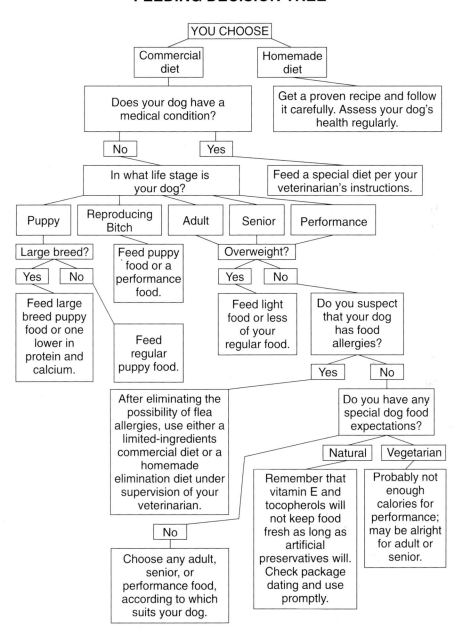

YOU CHOOSE

Commercial diet

Homemade diet

Does your dog have a medical condition?

Get a proven recipe and follow it carefully. Assess your dog's health regularly.

No

Yes

In what life stage is your dog?

Feed a special diet per your veterinarian's instructions.

Puppy

Reproducing Bitch

Adult

Senior

Performance

Large breed?

Feed puppy food or a performance food.

Overweight?

Yes

No

Yes

No

Feed large breed puppy food or one lower in protein and calcium.

Feed regular puppy food.

Feed light food or less of your regular food.

Do you suspect that your dog has food allergies?

Yes

No

After eliminating the possibility of flea allergies, use either a limited-ingredients commercial diet or a homemade elimination diet under supervision of your veterinarian.

Do you have any special dog food expectations?

Natural

Vegetarian

No

Choose any adult, senior, or performance food, according to which suits your dog.

Remember that vitamin E and tocopherols will not keep food fresh as long as artificial preservatives will. Check package dating and use promptly.

Probably not enough calories for performance; may be alright for adult or senior.

Glossary

AAFCO Association of American Feed Control Officials, an agency that develops regulations and guidelines for the production and labeling of animal feeds. If you want to read the official AAFCO definitions of dog food ingredients and package labeling, you can receive the *Official Publication*, updated each year, by contacting Charles P. Frank, AAFCO Treasurer, at the Georgia Department of Agriculture, Plant Food, Feed and Grain Division, Atlanta, GA 30334, 404-656-3637. Price for the 1997 edition was $25.

Adaptive thermogenesis Energy needed to maintain internal stability and body temperature.

Additive Two types of additives are used. Nutritional additives include vitamins, minerals, fats, and amino acids, often added in pure form for better availability and stability. Other additives provide some benefit other than nutrition, such as antioxidants (BHA, BHT, and mixed tocopherols) to prevent rancidity of fats in the food, chemical preservatives (propylene glycol, sorbic acid, and potassium sorbate) to prevent mold and bacterial growth, flavoring agents (garlic, onion, and many chemicals), or colorings.

Adulterated Food containing any part of a diseased animal or any filthy, putrid, or decomposed substance; packed or held under unsanitary conditions in which it may have been contaminated with filth or rendered injurious to health.

Alfalfa meal The above-ground portion of the alfalfa plant, which is sun cured and finely ground.

All (or 100%) In reference to the name of a food, i.e., All Beef Kibble, it means the product can contain only the named ingredient plus flavorings, preservatives, vitamins, minerals, and water.

All stages Indicates that the food will provide adequate nourishment for puppies, pregnant or nursing females, or adults.

Amino acids The organic building blocks that create protein.

Animal Ingredients coming from cattle, pigs, sheep, goats, horses, poultry, or fish.

Animal by-product meal The rendered product from animal tissues, exclusive of any added hair, hoof, horn, hide trimmings, manure, and stomach and rumen contents, except in such amounts as may unavoidably occur in good processing practices.

Animal fat Fatty acids obtained in the commercial process of rendering tissue from mammals or poultry, with no addition of free fatty acids. If an antioxidant is used, the common name or names must be indicated, followed by the words "Used as a preservative."

Anorexia Lack of appetite.

Antioxidants Substances that aid in preserving foods by retarding deterioration, rancidity, or discoloration; at the cellular level, substances that help protect the body against cell damage from free radicals.

Artificially dried Moisture having been removed by other-than-natural means.

As fed The food in the form actually fed to the dog, including whatever percentage of water exists in the food.

Ash The total mineral content of a pet food; the residue remaining after a food sample is burned at a temperature of 600°C for two hours, composed of calcium, phosphorus, potassium, magnesium, and other essential minerals.

Aspic A solid or semisolid dressing produced by mixing a gelling agent(s) with broth or water and/or common seasonings or flavor enhancer(s). If the aspic or gel is characterized as a meat, poultry, or fish aspic or gel, it must contain an extract or essence of meat, poultry, or fish in an amount sufficient to characterize it as such.

Avidin Enzyme in raw egg white that interferes with absorption of biotin, an important B complex vitamin.

Balanced A term applied to a food having all known required nutrients in proper amount and proportion based upon recommendations of recognized authorities in the field of animal nutrition for a given set of physiological animal requirements, such as maintenance or growth.

Beef Clean flesh limited to striated muscle from slaughtered cattle.

Beet pulp Dried residue from sugar beets.

BHA Butylated hydroxyanisole, a chemical preservative.

BHT Butylated hydroxytoluene, a chemical preservative.

Biological value The percentage of absorbed protein that is retained by the body or the amino acids actually converted into body tissue.

Biscuit A blended and baked dry food, shaped into a biscuit form.

Blending To mingle or combine two or more ingredients of feed.

Bone Skeletal part of vertebrates.

Boneless The flesh resulting from removal of bone from accompanying flesh by means of knife separation.

Dogs will burn more calories in this sort of weather.

Bone meal Dried and ground sterilized product resulting from cooking undecomposed bones. Fat, gelatin, and meat fiber may or may not be removed.

Brand name Any word, name, symbol, device, or any combination thereof identifying the commercial feed of a distributor and distinguishing it from that of others.

Brewer's rice A dried, extracted residue of rice resulting from the manufacture of malt or beer, allowed to contain up to 3 percent pulverized, dried, spent hops.

Brown rice Unpolished rice after the kernels have been removed.

By-products Cuts of meat or animal parts derived from the human food industry that are not used for human consumption; can include organ meats, blood, bone, brain, and tongue, pretty much anything but the stomach and intestinal contents.

Calorie The amount of heat energy necessary to raise the temperature of one gram of water from 14.5°C to 15.5°C.

Canned A term applied to a food that has been processed, packaged, sealed, and sterilized for preservation in cans or similar containers.

Cereals Grains, including wheat, barley, oats, rice, rye, maize, sorghum; used as a source of energy and protein, all similar in their nutrient values.

Chemical Chemical ingredients can include supplements and additives such as vitamins, minerals, colorings, flavorings, and preservatives such as BHA, BHT, ethoxyquin, vitamin C, and vitamin E.

Chemical score (biological score) An index comparing the amino acid composition of a given protein source with the amino acid pattern of a reference protein of very high quality, usually egg (given a score of 100). The essential amino acid in the shortest supply in the test protein is called the limiting amino acid. The percentage of that amino acid present determines the score.

Chicken Clean flesh and skin with or without bones, exclusive of feathers, heads, feet, and entrails.

Chicken by-product meal Ground chicken parts consisting of necks, feet, intestines, and undeveloped eggs, exclusive of feathers.

Chicken meal Chicken that has been ground or otherwise reduced in particle size.

Chunk A semimoist food extruded and cut into pieces like sausage.

Chunk style Canned food blended to a uniform mass and then extruded into chunks.

Cleanings Chaff, weed seeds, dust, and other foreign matter removed from cereal grains.

Colorings Added for consistent product appearance, as colors of natural ingredients can vary, or to distinguish between flavors in a multiparticle food.

Complete and balanced A food that contains all the essential nutrients at levels that meet a pet's requirements.

Complete food A nutritionally adequate food meant to be fed as the sole ration and capable of maintaining life without any additional substance other than water.

Corn bran The outer coating of the corn kernel without the starchy part of the germ.

Corn germ meal (dry milled) By-product of the dry milling process used in the manufacture of corn meal, corn grits, or other corn products, consisting of the ground corn germ with the oil removed.

Corn gluten By-product of the wet milling process used in the manufacture of corn starch or corn

syrup, consisting of the remains of shelled corn after most of the starch, gluten, and germ have been removed.

Corn gluten meal Dried corn gluten.

Corn syrup Concentrated juice derived from corn.

Cracked Particle size reduced by a combined breaking and crushing action.

Crude The amount of a nutrient measured by laboratory equipment, with no guarantee that the nutrient is in a form usable by the dog.

Digestibility coefficient The proportion of the consumed nutrient that is actually available for absorption and use by the body.

Digestible energy The actual amount of food that can be digested and absorbed by the dog.

Digests Liquefied or powdered fats and animal tissues sprayed

Just because a dog is an adult doesn't mean it doesn't want to play.

onto dry foods to enhance palatability.

Distributed by Indicates that the named company distributes a food actually manufactured by another company.

Dry matter An assessment of food with the moisture removed, useful in comparing percentages of different nutrients among several foods.

Eclampsia Medical condition caused by calcium deficiency in the lactating bitch.

Economy A low-priced food with lower-quality ingredients, including soy. Crude protein less than 19 percent, crude fat less than 8 percent, with less than 75 percent digestibility (from *Good Dog!* magazine).

Elimination diet A diet composed of limited novel ingredients, used to determine food allergies.

Emulsifier A material capable of causing fats or oils to remain in liquid suspension.

Essential amino acid The ten amino acids that cannot be produced by the body and must be provided from outside sources.

Expanded A dry food consisting of small, porous nuggets.

Extruded A blended dry food forced through a machine and cut to form it into various sizes and shapes.

Fat A concentrated source of energy, made up of fatty acids.

Fat-soluble vitamins Vitamins A, D, E, and K.

Feeding oatmeal By-product of the manufacture of rolled oats or rolled oat groats, consisting of broken oat groats, oat groat chips, and floury portions of oat groats, with no more than 4 percent crude fiber.

Fines Any materials that will pass through a screen whose openings are smaller than the specified minimum crumble size or pellet diameter; the tiny particles of food that break off of expanded or kibbled food in the process of manufacture and transport, creating a lumpy powder at the bottom of the bag.

Fish meal Clean, dried, ground tissue of undecomposed whole fish and/or fish cuttings; with or without extraction of part of the oil.

Fixed formula diet A food in which ingredients do not change in response to market prices.

Flakes An ingredient rolled or cut into flat pieces with or without prior steam conditioning.

Flavor Used in labeling, the word flavor (Beef Flavor Dog Food) may be used only if the food contains enough of the named flavor to be recognized by the dog; ingredient name used with a modifier (Liver Dinner or Beef Cakes) means the food is made from at least 25 percent of the named ingredient; ingredient name used without a modifier (Towser's Turkey) means the food contains at least 95 percent of the named ingredient.

Free choice (ad libitum) Method of feeding in which food is left available to the dog at all times.

Free radicals Unstable oxygen molecules produced during natural metabolism, which can trigger potentially damaging chemical reactions in the body in a process called oxidation.

Gastric dilation-volvulus (bloat) Condition in which the dog's stomach fills with gas, swells, and often twists, rapidly compromising circulation and breathing; a medical emergency.

Germ The embryo found in seeds and frequently separated from the bran and starch endosperm during the milling.

Gluten The tough, viscid, nitrogenous substance remaining when the flour, wheat, or other grain is washed to remove the starch.

GRAS Abbreviation for the phrase generally recognized as safe. A substance that is generally recognized as safe by experts qualified to evaluate the safety of the substance for its intended use; ethoxyquin is a GRAS substance.

Gravy A multiple-component fluid dressing or topping consisting of a combination of one or more ingredients imparting special characteristics or flavors. It may be formulated separately and added to another ingredient or combination of ingredients. If the gravy is characterized as a meat, poultry, or fish gravy, it must contain an extract or essence of meat, poultry, or fish in an amount sufficient to characterize it as such.

Gross energy The total energy included in a food but not necessarily capable of being digested and absorbed by the animal.

Growth A life stage designation meaning the food is suitable for nourishing puppies.

Guaranteed analysis Nutrient guarantees required to be on the label as crude protein (minimum), crude fat (minimum), crude fiber (maximum), and moisture (maximum), determined by laboratory assay.

Information panel Portion of the label containing the guaranteed analysis, list of ingredients, nutrition adequacy statement, daily feeding guidelines, and name and address of manufacturer.

Kernel A whole grain.

Kibble A blended and baked dry food, broken into random chunks.

Kibbled Cracked or crushed baked dough or extruded feed that has been cooked prior to or during the extrusion process.

Kilocalorie (kcal) The most commonly used unit of measure in the United States, equal to 1,000 calories.

Lard Rendered fat of swine.

Life stage information Designation required on the label, indicating the food is nutritionally suitable for growth (puppies), maintenance (adults), reproduction (pregnant and nursing females), or all stages.

List of ingredients All the materials making up the food, listed in descending order of predominance by weight.

Maintenance A life stage designation indicating the food is suitable for nourishing adults.

Maintenance energy requirement (MER) Amount of energy used by an adult animal at room temperature, expressed as kilocalories per kilogram of body weight per day (kcal/kg/day).

Manufactured by Indicates the named company makes its own foods and thus exerts its own quality control.

Manufactured for Indicates another company actually makes the food on behalf of the named company.

ME (metabolizable energy) The amount of energy in a pet food, measured in kilocalories, that is available for utilization by the animal's metabolism, as determined by feeding trials.

Meal An ingredient that has been ground or otherwise reduced in particle size; a dry food in flakes resembling cereal.

Meal-induced thermogenesis The heat produced following consumption of a meal; the energy needed to digest, absorb, and store nutrients.

Meat Any species of slaughtered mammal; the clean flesh derived from slaughtered mammals and limited to that part of the striated muscle that is skeletal or is found in the tongue, diaphragm, heart, or esophagus, with or without the accompanying and overlying fat and the portions of the skin, sinew, nerve, and blood vessels that normally accompany the flesh.

Meat and bone meal The rendered product from mammal tissues, including bone, exclusive of blood, hair, hoof, horn, hide trimmings, manure, and stomach and rumen contents, except in such amounts as may unavoidably occur in good processing practices.

Meat by-products Nonrendered clean parts, other than meat, derived from slaughtered mammals; includes, but is not limited to, lungs, spleens, kidneys, brains, livers, blood, bone, partially defatted low-temperature fatty tissue, and stomachs and intestines freed of their contents; does not include hair, horns, teeth, and hooves.

Meat meal Rendered product from mammal tissues, exclusive of any added blood, hair, hoof, horn, hide trimmings, manure, and stomach and rumen contents except in such amounts as may unavoidably occur in good processing practices.

Meat/meat products Indicates ingredients come only from cattle, hogs, sheep, or goats; other animal ingredients must be named specifically.

Metabolism The sum of all physical and chemical processed involved in living cells, including assimilating food and providing energy.

Microingredients Vitamins, minerals, antibiotics, drugs, and other materials normally required in small amounts and measured in milligrams, micrograms, or parts per million (ppm).

Minerals Essential inorganic elements used by the body in varying amounts for bone and tissue development, maintenance of body fluids, and prevention of anemia.

Misbranded Product bearing a false, misleading, or incomplete label.

Monogastric omnivore An animal having one stomach and eating a variety of meats, grains, and vegetables.

Mouth feel The size, shape, texture, and density of a food, all important in how appealing the food is when eaten.

Natural Minimally processed and free of chemical additives and preservatives, remaining close to how it occurs in nature; the actual statement must include a disclaimer such as, "Natural ingredients plus essential vitamins and minerals," and product may not contain artificial flavors or colors, or artificial preservatives.

Net energy Energy available to the animal for maintenance of body tissues and productive needs such as physical work, growth, gestation, and lactation.

Nutrient A feed constituent in a form and at a level that will help support the life of an animal. The chief classes of feed nutrients are proteins, fats, carbohydrates, minerals and vitamins.

Nutritional adequacy statement One of two statements must be on the label. "This product is formulated (calculated) to meet the AAFCO dog food nutrient profile for [whatever life stage]," meaning the food has been assayed in the laboratory; or "Nutritionally complete and balanced for [whatever life stage] as substantiated through testing in accordance with AAFCO procedures," meaning the food has undergone feeding trials.

Offal Material left as a by-product from the preparation of some specific product, less valuable portions, and the by-products of milling.

Organic Grown or raised without chemicals, fertilizers, or pesticides.

Palatability Assessment of a food's appeal to the taste buds.

Performance Similar to super-premium foods, but with at least 30 percent crude protein and 20 percent fat, with 82 to 86 percent digestibility (from *Good Dog!* magazine).

Polydipsia Increased thirst and drinking.

Polyuria Increased urination.

Popular Brands marketed regionally or nationally and sold in supermarkets; most are variable formulas (definition from Iams).

P is for Poodles parading in the park with their people.

Poultry The clean flesh and skin with or without bone, exclusive of feathers, heads, feet, and entrails.

Poultry by-product meal Consists of the ground, rendered, clean parts of the carcass of slaughtered poultry, such as necks, feet, undeveloped eggs, and intestines, exclusive of feathers, except in such amounts as might unavoidably occur in good processing practices

Poultry by-products Consist of nonrendered clean parts of carcasses of slaughtered poultry such as heads, feet and viscera, free from fecal content and foreign matter except in such trace amounts as might unavoidably occur in good factory practice.

Poultry fat (feed grade) Primarily obtained from the tissue of poultry in the commercial process of rendering or extracting. If an antioxidant is used, the common name or names must be indicated, followed by the word preservative(s).

Powdered cellulose Purified, mechanically disintegrated cellulose prepared by processing alpha cellulose obtained as a pulp from fibrous plant materials . . . in other words, sawdust.

Premium National or regional brands available only through pet supply stores, feed stores, or veterinarians, using fixed formulas (definition from Iams); at least 21 percent crude protein, and 10

percent crude fat, using good protein sources with good digestibility, though some may contain soy, with 82 to 86 percent digestibility (from *Good Dog!* magazine).

Preservative A substance added to protect, prevent, or retard decay, discoloration, or spoilage under conditions of use or storage.

Principal/main display panel That part of the label most likely to be displayed or presented under normal and customary conditions of display for retail sales. It must include the product name, the total amount of food in the package, and the statement that the product is dog food.

Protein Complex combinations of amino acids, essential for growth and repair of soft body tissues and bone development.

Ration type Canned food ground and blended into a uniform semi-solid.

Raw Not altered by cooking or processing.

Regular Moderately priced foods with moderate-quality ingredients, including soy. Crude protein is less than 19 percent, crude fats at least 7 percent. Found most at supermarkets. Less than 75 percent digestibility (from *Good Dog!* magazine).

Rendering The process of cooking animal tissues at high temperatures to separate the fat from the protein.

Resting metabolic rate (RMR) The amount of energy expended while sitting quietly in a comfortable environment several hours after a meal or physical activity.

Ribbon A semimoist food formed by alternating red and white ribbons in chunks to resemble pieces of meat marbled with fat.

Rolled Changing the shape and/or size of particles by compressing them between rollers.

Sauce A multiple-component, fluid dressing or topping consisting of a combination of one or more ingredients imparting special characteristics or flavors. It may be formulated separately and added to another ingredient or combination of ingredients.

SCFAs (short-chain fatty acids) The result of bacterial fermentation of fiber in the large intestine.

Shorts Fine particles of bran, germ, flour, or offal from the tail of the mill from commercial flour milling.

Social facilitation The canine characteristic of eating more in the presence of members of its pack, whether canine or human.

Soybean meal Obtained by grinding the flakes remaining after removal by a solvent extraction process of most of the oil from dehulled soybeans.

Stabilized To retard degradation of ingredients (the process used to be specified).

Stew Chunked meat with the addition of peas, chopped carrots, and maybe other vegetables.

Super-premium High-quality sources of protein and energy, with crude protein more than 23 percent and crude fat at least 14 percent. It contains no soy. Sold at feed stores and pet supply stores. *Good Dog!* magazine sometimes breaks this category down into two subcategories, with Super-premium I being higher in fat than Super-premium II. It has 80 to 85 percent digestibility (from *Good Dog!* magazine).

Tankage Residues from animal tissues, including bones and exclusive of hair, hooves, horns, and contents of the digestive tract.

Tocopherols A chemical preservative with no restrictions.

Variable formula diet A food in which ingredients change in response to market price, with changes not necessarily reflected on the label.

Viscera All the organs in the great cavity of the body, excluding contents of the intestinal tract.

Vitamins Organic compounds required for normal life functions including growth, development, and reproduction; for maintaining the balance between constructive and destructive cell changes; and for helping to resist disease.

Voluntary muscular activity Movement, such as walking or running.

Water-soluble vitamins C and B complex. Absorbed passively in the small intestine, and excreted in the urine.

Useful Addresses and Literature

For your convenience, some contact information that may prove useful is included here. First is a list of telephone numbers for pet food manufacturers. If the food you use is not included here, look on the packaging for contact information. The majority of manufacturers include an 800 number somewhere on their label. This is not a complete list and is not intended to endorse or exclude any particular product or manufacturer.

Second is a listing of contacts for the many and various organized dog sports. This is not a complete list, but can certainly point you in the right direction, whatever sort of dog you may have.

Third is a bibliography of related periodicals and books.

Pet Food Manufacturers

Abady Dog Food 914-473-1900
Alpo (Friskies) 800-745-3402
Bench & Field (Martin's Feed Mills)
    800-525-4802
Best Feeds & Farm Supply
    800-245-4125

Bil-Jac Foods 800-321-1002
Bluebonnet Milling Co.
    405-223-3010
Breeder's Choice 800-255-4286
Cornucopia Pet Foods
    516-427-7479
Cycle (Heinz Pet Products)
    800-252-7022
Eagle Products 800-255-5959
Eukanuba 800-535-VETS
Farnam Pet Products
    800-548-2828
Friskies 800-745-3402
Fromm Family Foods
    800-325-6331

Dogs never outgrow their need for nutritious food.

Gravy Train (Heinz Pet Products)
800-252-7022
Happy Jack 800-326-5225
Hill's Science Diet 800-445-5777
Iams 800-535-VETS, 800-525-4267
Innova 408-261-0770
Joy 800-245-4125
Kal Kan 800-525-5273
Kibbles'n Bits (Heinz Pet Products)
800-252-7022
Kruse Grain & Milling (Country
Perfection) 800-854-0658
Mighty Dog (Friskies) 800-745-3402
Natural Animal 800-548-2899
Natural Life 316-232-7127,
800-367-2391
Nature's Recipe 800-843-4008
Nutro 800-833-5330
Old Mother Hubbard/Neura
800-225-0904
Ol' Roy (Wal-Mart house brand)
800-624-PETS
Pedigree 800-525-5273
Pet Pride (Delight Manufacturing)
800-632-6900
Precise Pet Products
800-446-7148
Proclaim Pet Products
800-279-8968
Pro Pac (Midwestern Pet Foods)
812-867-7466
Purebred Co. (American Nutrition)
800-383-2601
Purina 800-778-7462 (and for Pro
Plan 800-688-7387)
Regal Pet Foods 800-638-7006
Sensible Choice (Pet Products
Plus) 800-592-6687
Silver Hydrant 410-461-2233
Solid Gold 800-364-4863
Star Milling Co. 800-733-6455
Sunshine Mills 800-705-2111

Supreme Pet Food
800-279-8968
Triumph Pet Industries
800-331-5144
Vet's Choice 800-494-7387
Waltham USA 800-528-1838
Wysong 800-748-0188

Canine Sports Organizations and Other Useful Contacts

First, the major multibreed registries are listed, each of which sponsors a variety of canine events throughout the United States all through the year. Then, the sponsors are listed by the specific events.

AKC (American Kennel Club)
5580 Centerview Drive
Raleigh, NC 27606
Registers nearly 150 dog breeds

UKC (United Kennel Club)
100 Kilgore Road
Kalamazoo, MI 49001
Registers over 200 dog breeds as
well as mixed breeds

SKC (States Kennel Club)
P.O. Box 389
Hattiesburg, MS 39403
Registers over 200 dog breeds

ARBA (American Rare Breed
   Association)
P.O. Box 76426
Washington, D.C. 20013
Registers rare European and other
   breeds not represented by the
   other registries

There are also parent clubs for
each individual dog breed, as well as
for mixed breeds, but the addresses
for these would fill a book alone.
Contact the registries given above if
you desire further information about
a particular breed.

Next, contacts specializing in
specific events:

Agility
AKC and UKC sponsor agility

NADAC
HCR 2
Box 277
Saint Maries, ID 83861

USDAA
P.O. Box 850955
Richardson, TX 75085

Canine Good Citizen (CGC)
Program sponsored by the AKC,
   the only AKC program open to
   mixed breeds

Clever Canine Companions (CCC)
Mrs. Jane Sohns
140 Weidler Lane
Rothsville, PA 17543
Registry awarding versatility titles to
   pure or mixed breeds; send
   SASE for information

Conformation
AKC, ARBA, SKC, and UKC all
   sponsor conformation

Draft Work
Bernese Mountain Dog Club of
   America
Carol Evert
221 Greenland Avenue
Oconomowoc, WI 53066

International Federation of Sledding
   Sports
Glenda Walling
7110 N. Beehive Road
Pocatello, ID 83201

International Sled Dog Racing
   Association
Donna Hawley
P.O. Box 446
Nordman, ID 83848

International Weight Pull
   Association
Jim Allers
503 East Street
Spokane, WA 99203

Newfoundland Club of America
Working Dog Committee
Marge Parsons
2461 Overlook Drive
Walnut Creek, CA 94596

North American Skijoring & Ski
   Pulk Association
907-248-7344

St. Bernard Club of America
Working Dog Committee
Marge Parsons
2461 Overlook Drive
Walnut Creek, CA 94596

Earthdog (Terrier Trials/Digs)
AKC

Flyball, Scent Hurdles
North American Flyball Association
P.O. Box 8
Mt. Hope, Ontario L0R 1W0 Canada

Freestyle
Relatively new sport, with handler and dog performing choreographed routines to music

Canine Freestyle Federation
576 Jackson Road
Mason, NH 03048

Musical Canine Sport International
Sharon Tutt
16665 Parkview Place
Surrey, B.C. V4N 1Y8 Canada

Herding
AKC

American Herding Breeds
   Association
Linda Rorem
1548 Victoria Way
Pacifica, CA 94044

Australian Shepherd Club of America
6091 E. State Highway 21
Bryan, TX 77808

International Sheep Dog Society
A. Philip Hendry, C.B.E.
Chesham House
47 Bronham Road
Bedford MK40 2AA, England

USBC (United States Border Collie)
   Handlers Association
Francis Raley
Rt. 1 Box 174,
Crawford, TX 76638

Hunting
AKC

NAHRA
P.O. Box 1590
Stafford, VA 22555

NAVHDA
P.O. Box 520
Arlington Heights, IL 60006

UKC

Lure Coursing
AKC

American Sighthound Field
   Association
Vicki Clarke
P.O. Box 399
Alpaugh, CA 93201

Puppydog All-Stars K-9 Games
Sirius Puppy Training
2140 Shattuck Avenue, #2406
Berkeley, CA 94704

Road Trials
Dalmatian Club of America
Mrs. I. Fleming
4390 Chickasaw Road
Memphis, TN 38117

Schutzhund
DVG America
Sandi Nethercutt, Secretary
113 Vickie Drive
Del City, OK 73115

United Schutzhund Club of America
3704 Lemay Ferry Road
St. Louis, MO 63125

Search and Rescue

American Rescue Dog Association
P.O. Box 151
Chester, NY 10918

SAR Dogs of the United States
P.O. Box 11411
Denver, CO 80211

Temperament

American Temperament Test Society
P.O. Box 397
Fenton, MO 63026

Therapy

Delta Society
289 Perimeter Road
Renton, WA 98055

Foundation for Pet Provided
    Therapy
3809 Plaza Drive, #107-309
Oceanside, CA 92056

Therapy Dogs Inc.
P.O. Box 2786
Cheyenne, WY 82003

Therapy Dogs International
6 Hilltop Road
Mendham, NJ 07945

Water

Newfoundland Club of America
Water Work Secretary, Linda Rand
7481 South 3500 East
Salt Lake City, UT 84121

Portuguese Water Dog Club of
    America
Ms. Joan-Ellis Van Loan
99 Maple Avenue
Greenwich, CT 06830

WET DOG
Lonnie Olson
5307 W. Grand Blanc Road
Swartz Creek, MI 48473

Other Useful Contacts

AAFCO
c/o Georgia Department of
    Agriculture
Agriculture Building
Capitol Square
Atlanta, GA 30334

Food and Drug Administration
Center for Veterinary Medicine
7500 Standish Place
Rockville, MD 20855

Morris Animal Foundation
45 Inverness Drive East
Englewood, CO 80112
800-243-2345

National Animal Poison Control
    Center
University of Illinois College of
    Veterinary Medicine
2001 South Lincoln Avenue
Urbana, IL 61801
800-548-2423 or 900-680-0000 fee
    charged for crisis management

National Research Council
2101 Constitution Avenue N.W.
Washington, DC 20418
202-334-2000

Pet Food Institute
1200 19th Street N.W., Suite 300
Washington, DC 20036
202-857-1120

Bibliography

Dog Magazines

AKC Gazette
51 Madison Avenue
New York, NY 10010

Bloodlines
United Kennel Club
100 East Kilgore Road
Kalamazoo, MI 49001

Dog Fancy
P.O. Box 53264
Boulder, CO 80328
(subscriptions)

Dog World
29 N. Wacker Drive
Chicago, IL 60606

Front & Finish
H & S Publications
P.O. Box 333
Galesburg, IL 61402

Good Dog!
P.O. Box 10069
Austin, TX 78766

Off-Lead
204 Lewis Street
Canastota, NY 13032

Books for Further Reading

Alderton, David. *The Dog Care Manual.* Hauppauge, NY: Barron's Educational Series, Inc., 1986.

Association of American Feed Control Officials, Inc. (AAFCO), Official Publication (published annually). To purchase contact: Charles P. Frank, AAFCO Treasurer, Georgia Department of Agriculture, Plant Food, Feed and Grain Division, Atlanta, GA 30334 (404-656-3637).

Baer, Ted. *Communicating with Your Dog,* Hauppauge, NY: Barron's Educational Series, Inc., 1989.

Billinghurst, Ian, *Give Your Dog a Bone,* self-published by Ian Billinghurst in Australia. Available from Dog & Cat Book Catalog at 1-800-776-2665.

Bower, John and David Youngs. *The Health of Your Dog,* Loveland, CO: Alpine Publications, 1993.

Burger, I.H., ed. *The Waltham Book of Companion Animal Nutrition,* New York: Pergamon Press, 1995.

Case, Linda P. et al. *Canine and Feline Nutrition: A Resource for Companion Animal Professionals,* St. Louis, MO: Mosby, 1995.

Dye, Dan et al. *Short Tails and Treats from Three Dog Bakery.* Kansas City, MO: Andrews & McMeel, 1996.

Pinney, Chris C., DVM. *Caring for Your Older Dog.* Hauppauge, NY: Barron's Educational Series, Inc., 1995.

Pitcairn, Richard and Susan. *Dr. Pitcairn's Complete Guide to Natural Health for Dogs and Cats.* Emmaus, PA: Rodale Press, 1995.

Taunton, Stephanie J., and Cheryl S. Smith. *The Trick Is in the Training.* Hauppauge, NY: Barron's Educational Series, Inc., 1998.

Wegler, Monika. *Dogs: A Complete Pet Owner's Manual.* Hauppauge, NY: Barron's Educational Series, Inc., 1992.

Index

What you put into these growing bodies is crucial. While it is important to feed puppies a variety of ingredients, it is equally important to control their caloric intake.